THEMES TO REMEMBER

VOLUME 1

by Marjorie Kiel Persons

including

LYRICS FOR CLASSICAL MUSIC

by Marjorie Kiel Persons

A publication of
Sing 'n Learn Publishing
5404 Lafayette Dr
Frisco, TX 75035
(800)460-1973
singnlearn@singnlearn.com

Lyrics for Classical Music
by Marjorie Kiel Persons
PO Box 1809
Banner Elk, NC 28604
© 1998, 2000 Marjorie Kiel Persons. All rights reserved.
Used by permission

Parents and teachers should use their own discretion to determine the suitability of certain lyrics for their children. Children should be supervised in the learning process. Neither the author nor Classical Magic, Inc. shall have any liability nor responsibility for any inappropriate use of the contents of this book.

Visit our website at http://classicalmagic.net

InternationalStandardBookNumber: 978-0-9834084-0-6

Publisher
Sing 'n Learn Publishing

Book Design & Layout
Marjorie & Clyde Persons

Composer Portraits
George Ann Johnson

Illustrator
Philip Nellis

CD Recording Studio
The Loft Studio, Boone, NC

Announcer
Tim Greene

Vocalists
Robert Matthews
Loree Hodge
Amy Young
Jonathan Maness

Keyboards
Robert Matthews

Violins
Jessica Johnson

Trumpets
Brent Bingham

ACKNOWLEDGMENTS

Special thanks to the Banner Elk Elementary School in Banner Elk, NC, for allowing me to test my "classical music magic" in the classroom.

In particular, I wish to thank:

Principal Sherri Carreker, who made me feel welcome;

Teresa Taylor, who graciously shared her classroom children with me;

Ellen Stapleton, who welcomed me in her music classes;

and all the children, who expressed such great enthusiasm and eagerness to learn.

Thanks also to:

Larene DeVine, Dudley Gilmer, and Joy Tuggy for proofreading;

Alex DeVine for helping with Allegro notation of musical themes;

Robert Matthews for finding musicians, playing keyboard, and directing the singing;

and Clyde Persons, my husband, who spent many hours as project and business manager, computer specialist, graphics designer, encourager, and partner in **Classical Magic's** production of *Themes to Remember,* **Volume 1.**

Dedication

To my grandchildren:

Alex and Jessalyn DeVine

Seth and Robin Parker

Sean and James Quick

and

To all my students who, over the years, have helped me
find the magic to put into **Classical Magic.**®

About the Author

Love of music, children and teaching has shaped the teaching career of Marjorie Kiel Persons. She has taught in many classroom situations, from a one-room country school in western South Dakota (a school she attended as a child) to public, private and parochial schools in urban and semi-urban environments. She has taught in several regions of the U.S. as well as Venezuela, the Caribbean island of Aruba, and in southern Mexico. While she has taught liberal arts subjects to many age levels, her real love has been teaching music, particularly classical music, to preschool and elementary school children, both in the classroom and in private piano lessons. The enthusiastic response of children of all ages and in all teaching environments over the years has been a major factor in the writing of this book. The response of children to her music teaching continues to be a source of great personal satisfaction to her.

Marjorie Persons is a *summa cum laude* graduate of Macalester College in St. Paul, Minn. She later completed post-graduate studies at the University of Minnesota and Kean College in New Jersey. She has majors in Elementary, Secondary, Music, and Religious Education, as well as English Literature. She and her husband Clyde, an engineer, lived in Venezuela, Aruba, Egypt and Mexico in addition to several regions of the U.S. They currently live in the Blue Ridge Mountains of northwestern North Carolina.

About the Illustrator

Philip Nellis has been drawing for as long as he can remember. His drawing during Mrs. Persons' literature classes in Oaxaca, Mexico, called her attention to his talent. She is pleased to feature his delightful illustrations in *Themes to Remember* for **Classical Magic** ®.

About the Portrait Artist

A native of Oklahoma, George Ann Johnson has been an active artist for over twenty years. Having a strong natural talent, she has studied at the Danforth Museum of Fine Art and with numerous nationally and internationally recognized artists. She has received many awards for her wildlife art and other fine art works. Her devotion is to pencil and watercolor portraits.

Foreword

Music is magical, and classical music is especially so. Recent studies show that it enhances learning and boosts our intellect. We hear it even before we are born; we are just beginning to realize how important classical music is for the child's brain development. We know that it inspires us, soothes us, and nourishes our soul. Can you imagine a world without music?

Maybe you have wanted to listen to classical music but didn't know where to begin. Would you like to be able to tell Bach from Haydn and to recognize some of their most famous music? **Classical Magic®** can help you recognize themes from classical music and be able to recall the names of both composer and composition in a very short time. And it's fun!

Classical Magic® works for very young children as well as adults. These lyrics for classical music themes contain the name of both the composer and the composition. You'll be amazed at how quickly you begin to hear, all around you, the themes you've learned. You may recognize them on TV or radio ads, on your cell phone or computer, in cartoons and movies, or in restaurants and elevators.

Children love **Classical Magic®** because they can sing along with the best music mankind has composed. The abstract is made concrete for them. They interact with the music, learn it, and remember it. **Classical Magic®** inspires children to listen to classical music and to play it on an instrument.

Classical Magic® has been successfully tested with children from pre-school (ages 2 to 4) through high school. Their resulting love for, and recognition of, classical music was truly amazing.

Let **Classical Magic®** do its magic. You'll enjoy it, and your children will be convinced that they are child prodigies!

Watch for more volumes of *Themes to Remember* by **Classical Magic, Inc..**

How to Use *Themes to Remember* by CLASSICAL MAGIC, Inc.
(Including the author's simple and practical teaching suggestions)

Listen and Sing Along
Children learn by listening and repeating. That's the way they learn a language; music is an abstract "language." Children learn music more quickly and remember it much better if they can sing words with it. Play the CD while they look at the pictures in the book, while driving in the car, or while they are playing quietly. Older children like to read the words in the book and sing along with the CD.

Meet the Composers
Composers are listed by historical period. Younger children won't understand this, but older children can start to understand that music, literature, and art reflect the period in which they were produced. Show children the pictures of the composers, and say their names. Older children will enjoy reading about the composers.

Musical Terms
Many musical terms are explained and can be taught to children as they are ready for them. Terms are defined at the bottom of each page. They are also defined in the glossary in Appendix 2. Piano, a quiet little cat, and Forte, a rather noisy little dog, will accompany you through the book.

Games
- **Name That Classical Tune**
  The themes are recorded with and without lyrics so you can play "Name That Classical Tune." Throughout *Themes to Remember*, [00] is used to indicate CD track number "00." The <u>odd</u> numbered tracks are the themes <u>without</u> lyrics and the next <u>even</u> number identifies the track with the same theme <u>with</u> lyrics. For those who want to play the themes on a keyboard or other instrument, the themes are notated in Appendix 1.
- **Name the Composer**
  Point to the picture of a composer. A child may be asked to tell the composer's name and/or the name of one of his compositions.
- **Who Am I?**
  A child pretends to be a composer and gives progressively more clues until someone guesses his identity.

Art
- **Draw While Listening**
  Once children learn a short theme taught in *Themes to Remember*, they may like to hear a more complete recorded version of the selection. Since small children have a short attention span, drawing or painting while listening can keep them focused. The lyrics for the themes will often suggest ideas for illustrations, or students may use their own imaginations.
- **Portray the Mood**
  Since music is an abstract medium, children can be instructed to use abstract art to portray the feeling or mood of the music they hear.

Drama and Dance

- ### Story Plays
  Themes to Remember includes the stories of *Swan Lake, Peer Gynt in the Hall of the Mountain King, William Tell,* and *Danse macabre.* These are wonderful for little plays. Children have great imagination for acting, but they will need direction to control their enthusiasm and prevent chaos, as any teacher knows.

- ### Shorter Drama
  The lyrics of many themes lend themselves to a miniature drama. Suggested are: Haydn's *"Surprise"* Symphony, Bach's Toccata and Fugue in D minor, Schubert's *Trout* Quintet, Schumann's *Happy Farmer,* and Brahms' *Lullaby.*

Movement

- ### Marching
  Children love to march. Give them a drum or a small flag to wave, and let them keep the beat to Sousa's marches. Also good for marching are Gounod's *Funeral March of a Marionette,* Bizet's *Toreador,* and the *William Tell* Overture by Rossini.

- ### Conducting - Rhythm Instruments
  Use a recorded version of Beethoven's Fifth Symphony, and let the children pretend they are conductors.
  Many selections are suitable for using rhythm instruments. Have children choose the type of instrument they think is suitable for the music they hear.

- ### Dance
  Children love "free expression" in dance, but they can also learn structured movement. Both the minuet and waltz are in triple meter. Children can easily learn this by counting - one, two, three - as they step in place or walk. When they are comfortable with this, tell them to accent the first beat - ONE, two three. Soon they will have the basic step for the minuet and the waltz.

  The lyrics for Handel's Minuet from *The Royal Fireworks Music* contain directions for a dance. The "hand" hold is actually an "arm" hold, from the elbow to the hand. The music is slow and the directions are easy to follow.

  Chopin's waltzes are very fast, made for listening, not for dancing. Strauss waltzes are more suitable for dancing, but they are still quite fast. Bizet's *Habanera* is a Cuban dance. Children love to move to this Spanish rhythm. Castanets add color.

Keep a sense of humor and a light-hearted attitude. You don't need to push children to learn classical music. They know quality when exposed to it. They'll be very excited to sing along with Bach, Beethoven, Brahms, and the rest of the best. Be sure that children understand that the composers did not write the lyrics. (The words from Handel's *He Shall Feed His Flock* come from the Bible). The lyrics are a means to learning and enjoying classical music. When children know the musical themes, they enjoy listening to extended recordings of classical music.

If you are interested in a lighthearted coverage of classical music written in a humorous style, I recommend *Classical Music for Dummies* (with CD) by David Pogue and Scott Speck.

Themes To Remember, *Volume 1*

BAROQUE

Vivaldi
Bach
Handel

CLASSICAL

Haydn
Boccherini
Mozart
Beethoven
Schubert

ROMANTIC

Rossini   Brahms
Mendelssohn   Saint-Saëns
Chopin   Bizet
Schumann   Tchaikovsky
Gounod   Dvořák
Strauss   Grieg

MODERN

Debussy
Rachmaninoff
Sousa
Elgar

Table of Contents

Contents

Contents

Contents

THEMES TO REMEMBER

VOLUME 1

TIMELINE OF COMPOSERS

Giving a date to a period of history is always approximate. Some periods of music arrived earlier in one part of Europe than in another, and some composers spanned more than one period. The following is by no means a complete list of classical music composers. However, the most familiar names are included. The composers included in **CLASSICAL MAGIC's** *Themes to Remember,* **Vol. 1** appear in bold type.

BAROQUE PERIOD (c.1600 – 1750)

PACHELBEL, Johann	(1653 - 1706)
CORELLI, Arcangelo	(1653 - 1713)
ALBINONI, Tomaso	(1671- 1750)
VIVALDI, Antonio	(1678 -1741)
MOURET, Jean Joseph	(1682 - 1738)
BACH, Johann Sebastian	(1685 - 1750)
HANDEL, George Frideric	(1685 - 1759)

CLASSICAL PERIOD (1750 - 1820)

GLUCK, Christoph	(1714 - 1787)
HAYDN, Franz Joseph	(1732 - 1809)
BOCCHERINI, Luigi	(1743 - 1805)
MOZART, Wolfgang	(1756 - 1791)
BEETHOVEN, Ludwig van	(1770 - 1827)
SCHUBERT, Franz	(1797 - 1828)

ROMANTIC PERIOD (1820 - 1900)

WEBER, Carl Maria von	(1786 - 1826)
ROSSINI, Gioachino	(1792 - 1868)
BERLIOZ, Hector	(1803 - 1869)
MENDELSSOHN, Felix	(1809 - 1847)
CHOPIN, Frédéric	(1810 - 1849)
SCHUMANN, Robert	(1810 - 1856)
LISZT, Franz	(1811 - 1886)
WAGNER, Richard	(1813 - 1883)
VERDI, Giuseppe	(1813 - 1901)
GOUNOD, Charles	(1818 - 1893)
SUPPÉ, Franz von	(1819 - 1895)
OFFENBACH, Jacques	(1819 - 1880)
SMETANA, Bedrich	(1824 - 1884)
STRAUSS, Johann Jr.	(1825 - 1899)
BRAHMS, Johannes	(1833 - 1897)
BORODIN, Alexander	(1833 - 1887)
SAINT-SAËNS, Camille	(1835 - 1921)
DELIBES, Clement	(1836 - 1891)
BIZET, Georges	(1838 - 1875)
MUSSORGSKY, Modest	(1839 - 1881)
TCHAIKOVSKY, Peter	(1840 - 1893)
DVOŘÁK, Antonin	(1841 - 1904)
MASSENET, Jules	(1842 - 1912)
GRIEG, Edvard	(1843 - 1907)
RIMSKY - KORSAKOV, Nicholas	(1844 - 1908)
FAURÉ, Gabriel	(1845 - 1924)
PUCCINI, Giacomo	(1858 - 1924)

MODERN PERIOD   (1900 to Present)

DEBUSSY, Claude	(1862 - 1918)
RACHMANINOFF, Sergei	(1873 - 1943)
SOUSA, John Philip	(1854 - 1932)
ELGAR, Sir Edward	(1857 - 1934)
MAHLER, Gustav	(1860 - 1911)
STRAUSS, Richard	(1864 - 1949)
DUKAS, Paul	(1865 - 1935)
SIBELIUS, Jean	(1865 - 1957)
WILLIAMS, Ralph Vaughan	(1872 - 1958)
HOLST, Gustav	(1874 - 1934)
IVES, Charles	(1874 - 1954)
RAVEL, Maurice	(1875 - 1937)
FALLA, Manuel de	(1876 - 1924)
BARTOK, Béla	(1881 - 1945)
STRAVINSKY, Igor	(1882 - 1970)
PROKOFIEV, Sergei	(1891 - 1953)
ORFF, Carl	(1895 - 1982)
GERSHWIN, George	(1898 - 1937)
COPLAND, Aaron	(1900 - 1990)
KHACHATURIAN, Aram	(1903 - 1978)
SHOSTAKOVICH, Dmitri	(1906 - 1975)
BARBER, Samuel	(1910 - 1981)
CAGE, John	(1912 - 1992)
BERNSTEIN, Leonard	(1918 - 1990)

BAROQUE

<u>Forte and Piano Go Baroque</u>

(c. 1600-1750)

Performing for Royalty

Key Date – 1620
Pilgrims land at Plymouth Rock

THE BAROQUE PERIOD (c.1600 – 1750)

VIVALDI, Antonio   **(1678 - 1741)**
BACH, Johann Sebastian   **(1685 - 1750)**
HANDEL, George Frideric   **(1685 - 1759)**

In the **Baroque** (buh-ROKE) **Period**, music was written mainly for church or for royalty. The Baroque era was the beginning of almost all of the musical styles up to the present. It is the period that paved the way for all later classical music.

Bach wrote principally for the church. **Handel** also wrote for the church but some of his greatest works were written for the theater (**operas and oratorios**) and for royalty, especially King George I and King George II of England. King George I liked to go barge-riding on the Thames (temz) River that flows through London. He also liked to dance gavottes and minuets. King George II enjoyed celebrations and watching fireworks that got out of hand!

Baroque music takes a theme or melody and interweaves it in repeated layers. You can think of it as three or four people singing a round (like *Brother John*) many times with many variations.

Music in the Baroque Period had many frills and fancy ornaments. In music that means things like **trills** and **grace notes.** Music was ornate like the Baroque architecture. During this period the violin family reached its highest development and the violin became the queen of instruments.

Notice that the composers in the Baroque Period wore big wigs. The peasants and poor people could not afford the wigs, so those who could afford them became known as the "Big Wigs" – people who were considered more important than people with less money. Some men even used powder on their wigs, or plaster of Paris to hold it in place. (Perhaps that was the first hair spray!) In England some judges, bishops, and men in parliament still wear big wigs. Every time you see a composer with a big wig, you can be quite sure that he composed during the Baroque Period.

---

opera - a musical play with orchestra, chorus, solos, and people in costume who sing rather than speak their lines.
oratorio - a musical story, usually from the Bible, with soloists, chorus, and orchestra, but without costumes, action or scenery.
trill - a quick repeating of two adjacent notes.
grace note - an extra note played very quickly before the main note.

ANTONIO VIVALDI
(1678-1741)

Antonio Vivaldi (Vi-VALL-dee) had bright red hair, under his big wig and he became a priest. Guess what they called him. You're right - the "Red Priest." However, he didn't stay in the priesthood. Instead he devoted his life to composing and teaching music. He was a **virtuoso** violinist, and he taught violin in a girls' school in Venice, Italy. He composed music for the girls. He also organized concerts, performed by the girls, which drew audiences from all over Europe.

Vivaldi developed the **concerto** form that we know today. A concerto (con-CHAIR-toe) is a composition for orchestra and a solo instrument. It has three parts, or movements. Vivaldi always used the same pattern for the three movements:

  Fast -- Slow -- Fast.

Composers usually use the Italian words:

  Allegro -- Adagio --Allegro

The Four Seasons is Vivaldi's most famous composition. He composed a concerto for violin and orchestra for each of the four seasons. We shall begin our **Classical Magic®** by learning the main theme from the first movement of *Spring*. Note that, as in all concerto first movements, it is **allegro.**

Vivaldi published a sonnet (poem) in Italian to go with each **concerto** to explain the music. For the first movement of *Spring*, he explains that spring has arrived and the birds are singing. The brook murmurs and soft breezes blow. Then thunder and lightning bring a shower. The shower is soon over, and the birds begin to sing again.

---

virtuoso - a performer who excels on his or her musical instrument

---

Springtime's the best time of year!
All the snow and ice disappear,
Songs of birds falling on my ear.

Springtime's the best time of year!
All the snow and ice disappear,
Songs of birds falling on my ear.

[: This music is by Vivaldi,
   This music is by Vivaldi,
   Vivaldi brings music and good cheer! :]

JOHANN SEBASTIAN BACH
(1685 - 1750)

Many people consider Bach (BAHkh) the greatest musician who ever lived, and his family the greatest musical family the world has ever known. Johann (YO-hahn) Bach wrote more music than most composers ever think of writing. He also had more children (twenty) than most composers ever think of having! All of his children loved music and many became accomplished musicians. Several became famous composers. In Germany, where Bach was born, the name Bach became synonymous with "musician."

Before Bach was ten years old, his parents died and he went to live with an older brother. The brother taught Johann to play the clavichord, an instrument much like the piano. Once, his brother refused to let him use a big book of difficult music. Johann secretly took the book and copied it in his attic room by moonlight. Although Bach played many instruments, he was known primarily as a superb organist, one of the greatest who has ever lived. Bach was not appreciated as a great composer until a century after his death.

Bach also improvised (made up on the spot) a lot of music that was never written down. He composed choral, organ and instrumental music primarily for the church. Some of his greatest music was written for the organ. **The Toccata and Fugue in D Minor**, which we shall learn next, is an organ composition.

Toccata comes from the Italian word *toccare*, which means to touch. The keys are touched very quickly! You can think of a **fugue** as similar to a round in singing. An organist playing a fugue often has the theme going with both hands and feet simultaneously. A composition written in a **minor** key will usually sound sad or spooky. I'm sure you've heard the **Toccata and Fugue in D Minor** played in department stores at Halloween. You can hear it on *Fantasia* and *Phantom of the Opera*.

We will learn two themes from the **Toccata and Fugue in D Minor.** Next Halloween you can surprise your friends by telling them that they are listening to Johann Sebastian Bach.

Haunted house! Goblins gonna get you!
Haunted house! Here come the ghosts!
Haunted house! It's Johann!
Watch out, watch out, watch out!
It's Johann Sebastian BACH!

Johann Bach wrote this toccata;
He wrote fugues and some sonatas;
He wrote preludes and cantatas,
Minuets and some gavottes!
Boy, he sure did write a lottas!

toccata - keyboard composition played (touched) very fast.
fugue - like a round written for instruments.
sonata - a composition for one or two solo performers.
prelude - introductory music - to play beforehand.
cantata - composition for voices, usually for church.
minuet - courtly dance music in three beats.
gavotte - peasant dance music in quick four beats.
lottas - not a word - but you know what I mean!

GEORGE FRIDERIC HANDEL
(1685-1759)

Handel was born in Germany the same year as Bach. His father hoped he would be a lawyer, but Handel had such great musical talent that his father consented to let him study music. He studied organ, harpsichord, violin and oboe. By the time he was eleven, he was composing his own sonatas and church services.

Handel traveled to Italy to learn about opera and to study the music of Vivaldi and Corelli. After three years in Italy, Handel decided to travel to England. While Handel was in England, Queen Ann died. There was no English heir to the throne, so the English people had to look for a cousin in Germany to be the next king. George I was that king. He did not speak English, but Handel spoke German and had worked for George I when he lived in Germany. Handel was pleased to serve King George I again in England.

King George I loved Handel's music and asked him to compose special music for a royal water pageant down the Thames River in London. The king's party enjoyed the festivities on the royal barge while Handel and his orchestra played the *Water Music* from a barge that floated nearby. Many other boats and barges joined the festivities. King George liked Handel's music so much that he had it played three times. We will learn the theme for *Alla Hornpipe* from the *Water Music*.

Handel wrote many **operas** and **oratorios**. *The Messiah* is his most famous oratorio. He composed it in just twenty-three days. Solo singers, chorus and orchestra tell the story of Christ. All the words in the Messiah are taken from the Bible. We will learn themes for the *Hallelujah* **Chorus** and *He Shall Feed His Flocks* from *The Messiah*.

The *Music for the Royal Fireworks* was written for King George II to celebrate the peace treaty that ended the War of the Austrian Succession. There were feasts and balls, and there was to be a huge celebration in London with great fireworks and great music. Great music they had, but the fireworks display was much greater than planned. The scaffold for the fireworks caught on fire, everyone panicked, and nobody heard the rest of the music. The *Royal Fireworks Music* is one of Handel's best-loved works and has been heard many times since that ill-fated day. (We think King George's pants caught on fire!)

Water Music - Alla Hornpipe

Let's play the Hornpipe
For Handel's music,
His Water Music,
The Royal Music.

King George is having a ball,
He says, "Please come, one and all."
King George says Handel will play.
The royal barge is waiting
For your presence there!

Let's play the Hornpipe
For Handel's music,
His Water Music,
Great music!

Let's play the Hornpipe
For Handel's music,
His Water Music.

King George is having a ball,
He says, "Please come, one and all."
King George says Handel will play.
Come let your cares float away!
    Come hear the orchestra play,
    And let us dance a bourrée
    For the King's matinée,
    And you'll be "Queen (King) for a Day."

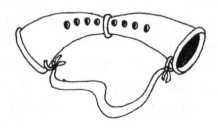

hornpipe - An English folk clarinet made with two ox horns. It gave its name to a dance related to the Irish jig. It features hopping and kicking of the feet. It became popular with sailors because it could be done in a small space without a partner.

The Messiah - *Hallelujah* Chorus

Handel
[9] & [10]

Handelujah, Handelujah,
The Messiah, The Messiah, Hallelujah!
Handelujah, Handelujah,
The Messiah, The Messiah,
Hallelujah!
For the Lord God **Omnipotent**
  reigneth,
Hallelujah, Hallelujah,
Hallelujah, Hallelujah.

The Messiah - He Shall Feed His Flock   [11] & [12]

He shall feed His flock like a shepherd,
And He shall gather the lambs with His arm,
With His arm......

The Messiah is an **oratorio.**

An **oratorio** is a musical story, usually from the Bible, with soloists, chorus and orchestra. All the words are sung but nobody dresses in costumes or acts the parts.

omnipotent - almighty or infinite in power.

13

Hail, King George,
Hear Royal Fireworks Music;
Hear Handel's music,
See rockets flare.
Beware, the fire's
Spreading everywhere!

Hail, King George,
Hear Royal Fireworks Music;
Hear Handel's music,
See rockets flaring.
Beware, the fire
Spreads everywhere!

Call the fire truck! Call the ambulance!
Call the fire truck! Call the ambulance!
  Call the fire truck,
I think King George's pants caught on fire!
We need water to douse the fire!
These Royal Fireworks,
Blazing fireworks,
Who lit this Fireworks Spectacular!

overture - an instrumental composition meant as an introduction to an opera, oratorio, or similar work. Some overtures stand by themselves, such as the *1812 Overture* by Tchaikovsky.

15

Royal Fireworks Music - Minuet

Handel
[15] & [16]

Bow to your partner.
Take her hand and turn around,
And then you clap your hands,
Clap your hands lightly,
Smile, she won't bite your nose!

Bow to your partner.
Take her hand and turn around,
And then you clap your hands,
Clap your hands lightly.
Smile! She's a lovely rose!

[: Dance, **minuet**,
  Dance, **tête-á-tête;**
  I won't forget---this minuet.
  Handel, Handel, wrote this minuet. :]

  (Repeat sign: [:   :])

Fireworks, Fireworks,
Dance up in the sky!
They have a ball before they fall,
Dance minuet!

Handel, Handel,
Play for the King's Ball.
Music to dance, songs for romance,
Dance minuet!

[: Stepping lightly, not too sprightly,
  But precisely, dance each measure.
  Oh, what pleasure!
  Careful! You stepped on my toe! :]

16

minuet - a slow, stately dance in triple meter (3 beats). It was introduced to the court during the Baroque Period and remained popular during the Classical Period. It evolved into the waltz of the Romantic Period.

tête-á-tête - face to face.

After the war comes **La Paix** day,
After the storm comes the sun's ray,
After the world's sadness,
After the world's madness,
Beautiful music from Handel for peace.
Ahhhhhh….

La Paix (pay) means "peace" in French.

Good Listening from the Baroque Period

The best way to learn to recognize the music of a period is to listen to it and learn the themes. I recommend:

Vivaldi

> *The Four Seasons*
> Concerto for Two Trumpets in C Major
> Cello Concertos
> Flute Concertos (James Galway)
> Guitar and Mandolin Concertos

Bach

> *Brandenburg* Concertos - 1 thru 6
> *Goldberg Variations*
> Organ Concertos
> Toccata and Fugue in Dm

Handel

> *The Messiah*
> *Water Music* Suite
> *Music for the Royal Fireworks*
> Organ Concertos
> Trio Sonatas

I recommend buying your child his or her own CD player (a nice gift for birthdays). You'll be amazed at how often children will listen to classical music if they have their own CDs and CD player.

When shopping for CDs of classical music, you may want to begin with collections of the best-known themes of classical music. Look for:

> The Top 100 Masterpieces of Classical Music 1685 - 1928
> The Most Beautiful Melodies of Classical Music
> Classical Moods Featuring the London Symphony Orchestra

There are ten CDs in each collection. These and other similar sets can be found at very reasonable prices.

CLASSICAL

Piano and Forte Go Classical

(1750 - 1820)

Forte Posing as George Washington

Key Date – July 4, 1776
Independence Day

THE CLASSICAL PERIOD (1750 -1820)

HAYDN, Franz Joseph   (1732 - 1809)
BOCCHERINI, Luigi   (1743 - 1805)
MOZART, Wolfgang Amadeus   (1756 - 1791)
BEETHOVEN, Ludwig van   (1770 - 1827)
SCHUBERT, Franz   (1797 - 1828)

Classical can be a confusing word. It refers both to a period of time and to a style of composition. In addition, all serious music by great composers is called classical music.

Classical period - the 1750 to 1820 musical period. Notice that Forte has a stern expression. This is the Age of Reason, sometimes called the Enlightenment. There are many rules to follow. Reason is more important than emotion.

Classical style - the style of music in the Classical Period.

Classical music - refers to music that is more complex and lasts longer than popular music. It is not just music from the Classical period. It includes music from four different periods: the Baroque, Classical, Romantic, and Modern. Each period has its own musical style. Music, art, and literature reflect the period in which they are produced.

The **Classical Period** was a time of change in ideas and feelings. Americans won their independence from England, and the social order in France was overthrown. In art, music, and literature, the people wanted a return to the simple beauties of nature and to clear thinking instead of fantasy. They were tired of the ornate Baroque style. There were very few prominent composers in the Classical Period.

Music in the **Classical Period** was written for the rich upper classes, the aristocracy, rather than for the church. The nobleman wanted to hear music that was more reserved, controlled, elegant, and tuneful than the Baroque style. There were rules about the form of the music and how the themes were to be developed. Rather than having themes interwoven, the soprano line (the highest-pitched melody) dominated the composition.

Classical Period music featured contrast. The dynamics shifted frequently between piano and forte. One finds wide-ranging melodies with wide spaces between the bass and soprano. There is contrast in mood even within a movement. This is very different from the **Baroque Period** music, which was based on the idea of unity by repeating a motive or a fugue subject over a long harmonic plan with fewer dynamic contrasts or wide register spaces.

Musical Forms of the Classical Period

The Classical sonata form was the mold for the Classical music. Written in two, three or four movements, it was a perfect vehicle for contrasts and surprises.

form - Form in music means a musical plan similar to an outline for a book. Forms were well defined in the Classical Period. We will consider only the <u>outline</u> form of the music, not the form <u>within the movements</u> of the music.

The **sonata, string quartet, symphony, and concerto** were the prominent forms in the Classical Period. To be a child prodigy (or an informed adult), you'll want to know how to tell them apart.

sonata - composition for only one or two instruments
      (usually) three movements   Fast Slow Fast

string quartet - composition for two violins, viola, and cello
      (usually) four movements   Fast Slow Minuet Fast

symphony - composition for a full orchestra
      (usually) four movements   Fast Slow Minuet Fast

      (**symphony** can also refer to the type of orchestra, i.e. a symphony orchestra)

concerto - composition for a full orchestra featuring a solo instrument
      (usually) three movements   Fast Slow Fast

A **movement** is a distinct part of a musical composition, like a chapter in a book. The musicians will usually stop completely between movements. **Don't clap** until the end of the last movement, or you may find yourself clapping alone.

Did you notice that there are more Fast than Slow movements? We usually get bored sooner with slow things, but we still want contrast or change because we also get bored if everything is fast! The classical composers worked out a balance. About the time we get tired of the Fast movement, they change to the Slow movement and give our minds a rest. Then, before we go to sleep, they wake us up again with a Fast movement!

SYMPHONY ORCHESTRA SEATING PLAN

FRANZ JOSEPH HAYDN
(1732 - 1809)

Joseph Haydn (HIGH-dn), or "Papa Haydn", as Mozart called him, is also called the "Father of the Symphony." His parents were amateur musicians who played several instruments and loved to sing. They recognized little Haydn's talent and sent him, when he was five, to live with a relative who taught music. Poor little Franz Joseph was not treated well, but he did receive excellent musical training. A boys' choir in Vienna accepted him when he was only eight years old. Again, the musical training was excellent, but he was often cold and hungry. Many times he sang in the streets to earn a few extra coins to buy food.

Better days were ahead for Haydn. Prince Esterhazy of Austria gave him a job as court musician. Although he was considered a "servant," he was treated well and was happy that he could devote himself entirely to music. He wrote most of his music for the court, since the Prince was his employer. His symphony orchestra performed his music for small audiences at court. Therefore, his symphony orchestra was much smaller than today's symphonies. His symphonies were also shorter than most symphonies of later composers. He wrote 104 symphonies compared to nine that Beethoven composed.

Haydn was famous and dearly loved all over Europe. He spent three years in London. While there, he wrote his twelve *London* symphonies. A favorite is **Symphony No. 94, (Surprise)**. It is said that the loud chord in the second movement was intended to awaken guests at the palace who drifted off to sleep during a concert after a big meal!

Movements of a symphony:

Movement one - Fast
Movement two - Slow
Movement three - Minuet or Scherzo
Movement four - Very fast

Haydn has a big surprise,
Go to sleep now, close your eyes.
Music soft and music sweet,
What a listening treat!

> Haydn has a big surprise,
> Go to sleep now, close your eyes.
> Music soft and music sweet,
> Jump up on your feet! SURPRISE!

[: Wake up, listen to the music
   Haydn wrote for you and me.
   But if you're going to go to sleep,
   Go home, go to bed and count your sheep! :]

For convenience, in this book **"Movement"** will be abbreviated Mvt.

scherzo - in Italian means "joke" and is rollicking as the name suggests.
Like the minuet, it has triple meter. (Count 1 -2 -3)

25

LUIGI BOCCHERINI
(1743 - 1805)

Boccherini (bok-a-REE-nee) was Italian (as you may have guessed) and was a very successful cellist and composer. Haydn knew him and admired him. His music, mostly chamber music, is beautiful. Musicians in his day usually played in small places (chambers) for small groups. The Infante Luis of Spain employed Boccherini as chamber-musician and composer, and Frederick Wilhelm of Prussia honored him with the title of "chamber-composer." He wrote more than 400 works including 90 string quartets, 125 string quintets (nearly all scored for 2 cellos rather than 2 violas), 54 trios, and 20 symphonies.

Boccherini's music will calm your nerves, soothe your soul, and make you thankful that God gave you ears for listening.

The **Minuet** on the CD is from his **String Quintet, Op. 13, No. 4**. It is a very popular piece. If you take violin or piano lessons, you'll probably play it sooner or later. The **syncopated** rhythm makes us want to dance.

---

syncopated - the weak beat is accented - jazz music uses it a lot.
If you think it sounds **jazzy**, it's probably **syncopated**!
If you are counting four beats to the measure, the first and third beats are usually the heavy beats.   ONE   two   THREE   four

To make it syncopated, count ----one   TWO   three   FOUR.

Op. stands for **Opus** which means a "work". Opus is used by composers and publishers to identify their works. The word is usually reserved for a collection of works of the same kind. Op. 13, No. 4 would mean that the music is No. 4 in Book 13.

String Quintet, Op. 13, No. 4 - Minuet

Oh, let's dance Boccherini's Minuet,
Written in a hurry for his mother's string quintet.
     Play it light, Luigi,
     Play it right Luigi,
Play tonight, Luigi, while we're still in love.

Oh, let's dance Boccherini's Minuet,
Written in a hurry for his mother's string quintet.
     Play it light, Luigi,
     Play it right, Luigi,
     Play tonight, Luigi, while we're still in love.

     Play it light, Luigi,
     Play it right, Luigi,
     Play it light, Luigi
     Play tonight, Luigi…….
       (D.C. al Fade Out)

WOLFGANG AMADEUS MOZART
(1756 - 1791)

Wolfgang Amadeus Mozart (MOHT-sart) is considered by many to be the greatest composer who ever lived. He produced music more easily than most of us write a letter. It came fully formed in his head, and he needed only to write it down. He could listen to complex music and later write it down totally from memory.

Mozart's father, also a musician, recognized his son's talent and provided him with early training. At the age of four, he composed a piano concerto. His sister Nannerl was also very talented. Papa Mozart thought he could make some badly needed money by taking his children on a tour of Europe to play concerts for royalty. In every country Mozart was called a "wonder child." His ability to **improvise** and to **sight read** astounded everyone who heard him. Although the children played brilliantly, the money they made hardly covered clothing and traveling expenses.

Mozart was born in Salzburg, Austria. As a young man, he moved to Vienna, the center of the classical music world. There he met "Papa Haydn." Haydn taught Mozart, and they became very good friends. Although Haydn was much older, he learned from the brilliant Mozart. He told Mozart's father, "I tell you before God, and as an honest man, that your son is the greatest composer that ever lived."

Mozart died very young, at age 35. Yet, in his short life, he composed volumes of music. His music is the ultimate example of the classical style. It is gracious, elegant and refined, yet it has a sense of divine inspiration. *Amadeus* means "beloved of God." How can we doubt it when we hear his music? Listen for the angels in the second movement of his **Piano Concerto No. 21**.

---

improvise - to make up new music on the spot.
sight read - to read and play music that one has never seen or practiced before.

Piano Concerto No. 21, Mvt. 2

Mozart
[23] & [24]

Songs of angel choirs
Floating all around us.
Songs Mozart wrote,
How they astound us.
Sing, Concerto 21,
Sing, Mozart sing!
Oh, you can be an angel, too!

Symphony No. 40, Mvt. 1   [25] & [26]

Symphony, Symphony Number Forty,
Wolfgang Amadeus Mozart.
Symphony, Symphony Number Forty,
Wolfgang Amadeus Mozart.
Lovely melody in minor,
Lovely melodies for children
Singing symphonies……
Sing out! Sing out!
Sing out, sing out,
    Symphony, Symphony Number Forty,
    Wolfgang Amadeus Mozart.

Symphony No. 40 is one of Mozart's last symphonies. The first theme is sure to linger in your mind. Once you know the theme, you'll be surprised how often you hear it.

LUDWIG van BEETHOVEN
(1770 - 1827)

Beethoven (BAY-toe-ven) also studied with Haydn, but not for long. He was unhappy with the restraints of the classical style of music; he wanted to make his own rules. He did just that in his later works, which really belong in the Romantic Period. **Symphony No. 5** is probably the most familiar of Beethoven's symphonies. The beginning notes, three short and one long, are simple yet powerful. Beethoven took a simple idea and turned it into a dramatic statement.

The last movement of his **Symphony No. 9** (which has the theme you will learn) uses a large choir to sing the *Ode to Joy*. No other composer in the Classical Period had ever used a choir in a symphony or made music sound so dramatic and exciting. Beethoven also broke the classical rules in the *Moonlight Sonata*. The usual pattern for a sonata is Fast - Slow - Fast. Beethoven begins the *Moonlight Sonata* with a very slow movement and continues with two fast movements.

Beethoven never married, which was probably just as well. He had a hot temper, was moody and independent. A genius can be difficult to live with! There are many stories of Beethoven's romances. One of the most fascinating is the "Immortal Beloved" mystery romance. After Beethoven died, three love letters were found in a drawer of his desk. In one letter he addresses the person as "Immortal Beloved." but there is nothing to tell us who she might be. There is no date or address given in the letters. The "Immortal Beloved" movie suggests some answers to the mystery, but they are only speculations.

Beethoven began to lose his hearing when he was only 31. This was a great tragedy for someone whose life was music. However, he continued to compose his sublime music. He was completely deaf when he composed the **Ninth**, his last symphony. In spite of this, he insisted on conducting the orchestra and chorus. At the end, he could not hear the applause. His friends had to turn him toward the audience for him to see the applause.

Beethoven knew that he was a genius. He refused to be humble before the nobility. He once told his patron, Prince Lichnowsky, "There are, and there will be, thousands of princes, but there is only one Beethoven."

30

Beethoven's Fifth, Beethoven's Fifth....
Beethoven's Fifth, Beethoven's Fifth, Beethoven's Fifth,
Beethoven's Fifth, Beethoven's Fifth, Beethoven's Fifth,
    Beethoven's Fifth   (Beethoven's Fifth)
    Beethoven's Fifth   (Beethoven's Fifth)
    Beethoven's Fifth, Fifth, Fifth.....

(Pretend that you are a great conductor of a symphony orchestra and "conduct" Beethoven's Fifth.)

[: Joyful, joyful sang Beethoven
As he wrote his Number Nine.
Though he could not hear the music
He knew that it was sublime. :]

Sonata No. 14 (*Moonlight*)

Beethoven, Beethoven, Beethoven
(repeat until melody begins – 19 times!)

Pale moonlight,
Soft moonlight,
Brings true love to me.

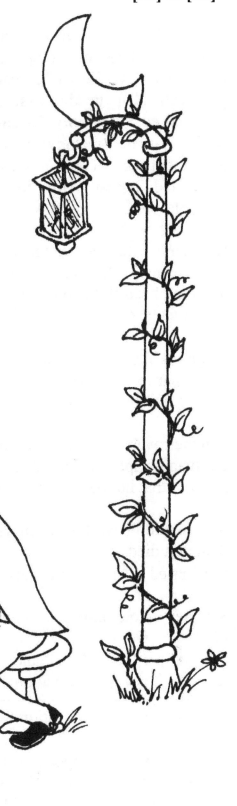

FRANZ SCHUBERT
(1797 - 1828)

Franz Schubert (SHOE-bert) has been called the "last of the Classical composers and the first of the Romantics." He wrote beautiful melodies, as you will hear in the first movement of his *Unfinished* **Symphony Number 8**. You might think that the melody belongs to a second movement as second movements are usually slow and lyrical. This melody is especially singable! It is one you won't forget. We don't know why he wrote only two movements. (Remember that a symphony usually has four movements!) Perhaps it was hard to write anything beautiful enough to follow the first two movements, or maybe he decided to read a good book and forgot to finish it!

Schubert liked parties with his friends. They sang and danced to Schubert's music, so the parties became known as *Schubertiads*. His friends called him "Mushroom." Maybe it was the hairdo. I never saw a mushroom with little wire-framed glasses!

Schubert was not famous in his lifetime. After he died, Schumann found some of his manuscripts and had them published. Gradually his fame spread, and people realized that he was a great composer.

Schubert idolized Beethoven. He was very sad when Beethoven died. Like Mozart, Schubert died very young, at 31. His dream was to be buried next to the master. He was buried as close to Beethoven "as could be arranged."

Schubert wrote only nine symphonies, but he wrote more than 600 songs (called *Lieder* in German). He also wrote many compositions for strings: **quartets, quintets and trios**. His Piano Quintet in A, (***The Trout***), for piano and strings is a favorite. It is a good CD to buy if you want to listen to more Schubert.

---

quartet - a composition for four instruments or voices.

quintet - a composition for five instruments. A **piano quintet** usually consists of a piano and a **string quartet** (which has two violins, one viola, and one cello).

trio - music written for three instruments or voices.

Symphony No. 8 – (*Unfinished*)

[: Schubert wrote symphonies
But he forgot to finish this one. :]

Yes, this one, oh

[: Schubert wrote symphonies
But he forgot to finish this one. :]

Piano Quintet in A - (*The Trout*)

When Schubert took me fishing,
We saw a giant rainbow trout.
But Schubert caught him easily
And let me pull him out.

The fish just flapped his finny feathers,
And then he flew up in the sky!
I know you believe my story.
I wouldn't tell a lie.

I know you believe his story.
He wouldn't tell a lie.

36

Good Listening from the Classical Period

Haydn

Symphony No. 101 in D major (*The Clock*)
Trumpet Concerto in E-flat major
Horn Concerto in D major
Cello Concerto in C major
Violin Concerto in G major

Boccherini

Cello Concertos
Flute Quintets
String Quartets

Mozart

Piano Sonata in C major, K. 545
Piano Sonata in B-flat major, K. 333
Piano Trios (Piano, violin, cello)
Clarinet Concerto in A major, K. 622
Violin Concerto No. 5 in A major K. 219
French Horn Concertos
Symphony No. 38 in D major (*Prague*), K. 504

Beethoven

Piano Concerto No. 2 in B-Flat
Piano Concerto No. 3 in C minor
Piano Concerto No. 5 in E-Flat
Violin Concerto in D major

Schubert

James Galway plays Schubert
Symphony No. 5 in B flat
Piano Quintet in A, (*The Trout*)

ROMANTIC

Piano and Forte Go Romantic

(1820 - 1900)

Forte Posing as Abraham Lincoln

Key Date – 1861 - 1865
Civil War

THE ROMANTIC PERIOD (1820 - 1900)

ROSSINI, Gioachino	(1792 - 1868)
MENDELSSOHN, Felix	(1809 - 1847)
CHOPIN, Frédéric	(1810 - 1849)
SCHUMANN, Robert	(1810 - 1856)
GOUNOD, Charles	(1818 - 1893)
STRAUSS, Johann Jr.	(1825 - 1899)
BRAHMS, Johannes	(1833 - 1897)
SAINT-SAËNS, Camille	(1835 - 1921)
BIZET, Georges	(1838 - 1875)
TCHAIKOVSKY, Peter	(1840 - 1893)
DVOŘÁK, Antonin	(1841 - 1904)
GRIEG, Edvard	(1843 - 1907)

The **Romantic Period** is very different from the **Classical Period**. The Romantic composer stressed the dignity and freedom of man, an idealized nature, the rustic village, the hero-warrior, warm lush sounds, and emotion. The **Classical Period** had stressed control of form and emotions.

The music of the **Baroque Period** was written mainly for the church or the court. The **Classical** composer wrote principally for the rich upper classes and the aristocracy. The **Romantic** composer wrote for the rising middle class. A classical composer needed to make a living from his music, by sales or by performance. Composers, such as Paganini on the violin and Liszt and Chopin on the piano, performed brilliantly for their audiences.

The forms of music were varied. Chopin wrote dazzling short works - waltzes, preludes, and études - for the piano. Liszt and Rubinstein wrote thundering concertos. Brahms wrote dark-hued symphonies. Tchaikovsky brought the ballet into prominence, and Berlioz included a waltz in his *Symphonie fantastique*. The waltz replaced the minuet. Symphonic poems (or tone poems) were popular. They described storms, sunrises, and life with idealized nature. Composers started using folk melodies in their music. New instruments and the improvement of existing instruments gave the orchestras a richer, warmer, more powerful sound.

Notice the great number of composers in the **Romantic Period. Classical Magic®** is waiting to introduce you to the wonder and beauty of Romantic music.

GIOACHINO ROSSINI
(1792 - 1868)

Gioachino Rossini (Ross-EE-nee) was a big man who loved to eat and enjoy life. His fellow Italians adored him and the beautiful melodies of his operas. The **Overture** to the *William Tell* opera is a concert favorite. The first theme is a lovely quiet melody played by the flutes. The second theme bursts in with a trumpet fanfare followed by a very fast melody that many people associate with "The Lone Ranger." However, you will know that Rossini wrote it for the *William Tell* **Overture**.

The Story of William Tell

The people of Switzerland were oppressed by an Austrian ruler named Gessler. To break the proud spirit of the Swiss, Gessler had mounted his cap on a pole in the public square and required each man to bow to the cap. William Tell refused to bow to anyone or anything. This made Gessler furious.

William Tell was noted for his great skill with the crossbow. Gessler thought of a cruel plan to bring him down. He ordered William Tell's young son to stand across the public square with an apple on his head. He ordered William Tell to shoot it off with one arrow, or his men would shoot the boy.

Gessler didn't believe that William Tell could hit the apple at such a distance. William took two arrows from his quiver, took careful aim, and split the apple in half, leaving his son unharmed.

Gessler asked Tell why he had taken two arrows from his quiver. William said, "If I had missed the apple and hurt my son, I would have killed you with the second arrow."

Gessler ordered William Tell led away to life in prison. However, Tell escaped. It is said that William Tell's arrow later killed Gessler and thus freed the Swiss from his tyrannical rule.

Rossini's *William Tell* **Overture** is a small **tone poem**, a poem in music rather than words. If possible, listen to a fully orchestrated version of the Overture. It begins with a beautiful slow section that depicts the rising of the sun over the Swiss mountains. A fast section follows in which we hear a storm. Then, on our Track 38, the quiet returns with a pastoral scene and a gentle mountain melody. On our Track 40, we hear the Swiss soldiers arrive with the Trumpet Fanfare.

William Tell Overture - Theme 1

Rossini
[37] & [38]

Rossini, Tell William Tell how he saved Switzerland
From the tyrant who ruled his land.

Rossini, Tell William Tell how his son
Stood so bravely with apple upon his head.

Rossini, Tell William Tell how with crossbow and arrow
His shaft hit the mark, apple fly!

Rossini, Tell William Tell how he saved Switzerland
From the tyrant who ruled his land….

William Tell Overture - Theme 2 - Trumpet Fanfare

[39] & [40]

[: William Tell, William Tell,
William Tell, Tell, Tell,
Rossini, Rossini, Rossini, ni, ni….
William Tell, William Tell,
William Tell, Tell, Tell,
Rossini, ni, ni, ni, William Tell! :]

The opera *William Tell* and the story above are based on a drama by Frederich
von Schiller, a German poet, dramatist, historian and philosopher.
opera - a musical play with orchestra, chorus, solos, and people in costume
who sing, rather than speak, their lines.

FELIX MENDELSSOHN
(1809 - 1847)

Felix Mendelssohn (MEN-dl-son) composed his famous *Wedding March* as background music for Shakespeare's play, *A Midsummer Night's Dream,* when he was seventeen. For many years, brides walked down the aisle to the music of Wagner's *Bridal Chorus.* At the end of the ceremony, after the groom kissed the bride, the happy couple left the church to the music of Mendelssohn's *Wedding March.* Many brides now choose music other than Wagner and Mendelssohn for their weddings.

Felix came from a prosperous family that nurtured his musical talent. He was born in Hamburg, Germany. His grandfather was Moses Mendelssohn, a famous **philosopher**. Felix was almost as talented as Mozart. Like Mozart, he could compose music fully formed in his head and then write it down. He also had a wonderful musical memory.

Mendelssohn liked to travel. His favorite foreign country was England and Scotland which he visited ten times. His Symphony Number Three is called the "Scotch" Symphony.

Mendelssohn is responsible for bringing Bach's music to light. Bach had been a famous organist, but he was not widely known outside of Germany in his own lifetime. After his death in 1750, his music was almost forgotten until Felix found it a century later and brought it to the attention of the world. Bach's music has been loved and played around the world ever since.

Mendelssohn composed wonderful symphonies and concertos. He also wrote an oratorio called *Elijah.* Remember that an oratorio is a musical story with chorus, soloists, and orchestra. It is usually based on the Bible.

Mendelssohn worked very hard. His health began to fail when he was only 35. He was very fond of his sister Fanny, a gifted composer and pianist. When she died unexpectedly, it was a great shock to Felix, and he died a few months later at the age of 38.

> **philosopher** - a person who ponders the meaning and value of life

A Midsummer Night's Dream – Wedding March

Mendelssohn
[41] & [42]

Oh, here comes the happy couple
Walking down the aisle,
Vows made to love forever,
Or at least for a while!

Mendelssohn's March, Mendelssohn's March
Midsummer Night, Midsummer Night
Midsummer Dream, Midsummer Dream

Here comes the happy couple
Walking down the aisle,
Vows made to love forever,
Or at least for a while!

FRÉDÉRIC CHOPIN
(1810 - 1849)

Frédéric Chopin (sho-PAN) was born in Poland. His mother was Polish and his father French. Frédéric was very unhappy with the grim circumstances in Russian-occupied Poland. He left when he was twenty and made his home in France for the rest of his life. However, he never forgot his Polish heritage. His music is full of the sounds of Polish national dances such as the mazurka and polonaise. His *Revolutionary* **Étude** and *Military* **Polonaise** reflect his nationalism and his distress with Russian occupation.

Chopin composed mostly short works for the piano. There are **preludes, nocturnes, waltzes, mazurkas, études, polonaises, impromptus,** and **sonatas**. He composed in many moods: tragic, sweet, dreamy, brilliant, heroic, fantastic and simple. He was the master of beautiful melody. Many of his melodies have been used in popular songs. Two of the best-known popular songs are:

Tristesse Étude - "No Other Love"
Fantasie-Impromptu - "I'm Always Chasing Rainbows"

Chopin was a brilliant pianist. He enthralled people with his wonderful music, and he was in great demand to perform. However, he was frail and sickly, so he limited his public appearances. Liszt is the only other composer who rivaled Chopin in his virtuosity. (A virtuoso is someone who can play amazingly well.)

---

prelude - a small concert piece based on a short motive.
motive - like a theme only much shorter.
theme - a musical idea that is developed in a composition.
nocturne - a dreamy composition appropriate for nighttime.
waltz - a lively couple dance with three beats in a measure.
mazurka - a lively Polish dance in triple meter (three beats).
étude - a study, a piece aimed at teaching a musical skill.
polonaise - a stately Polish processional dance in triple meter.
sonata - composition for one or two solo instruments in three movements.
impromptu - a composition of the Romantic Period. The name implies a somewhat casual origin of the piece in the composer's mind.

Grande valse brillante

Taa - Ta ta ta, ta ta ta, ta ta ta, ta ta ta, ta ta
Play, Chopin, play, valse brillante,*
Play, Frédéric, play, GO!
Won't you play every day
From June to May,
Valse brillante,*
Play, Freddy, play!

[: Play, Chopin, play, valse brillante,*
Play, Frédéric, play, GO!
Won't you play every day,
From June to May,
Valse brillante,* play! :]

* French pronunciation ignored for rhyming purposes!

ROBERT SCHUMANN
(1810 - 1856)

Robert Schumann was another tragic Romantic composer. He had periods of depression, tried to drown himself, and lived the last two years of his life in an asylum. Many people confuse Schubert and Schumann, but you can keep them straight. Just remember that Schubert had little wire glasses, looked like a mushroom, and liked to go fishing for trout. Schumann ran a shoe shop and sold yellow shoes to *The Happy Farmer*! They both died young; Schubert died when he was 31, while Schumann lived to be 46.

Most of the composers were child prodigies, and Schumann was no exception. (Maybe you are a child prodigy! It's a good word, even if it sounds suspicious!) Schumann's mother, however, thought Robert should study law; he obeyed and enrolled in law school. There he met Felix Mendelssohn and decided he liked the company of musicians better than lawyers.

Schumann decided to study piano with a very good teacher. His teacher had a daughter, Clara, who was also a prodigy. Schumann fell in love with her. Clara was nine years younger than Robert. Her parents were not anxious for her to marry him; in fact, they strongly opposed the marriage. Schumann persisted and eventually resorted to a lawsuit to win the right to marry her.

Robert and Clara Schumann helped the young Brahms by promoting his music and introducing him to other famous composers. They became good friends and remained so all their lives.

Robert became one of the greatest composers of his time. Clara became the greatest woman pianist of her generation. Clara also composed music, and her works are now being performed and recorded more frequently.

Schumann wrote mostly for solo piano, but his symphonies and concertos are also a good addition to your music collection.

The Happy Farmer

I love to sing,
I really love to sing!
I work all day just baling hay,
And sing, sing, sing. **(Fine)**

Oh dear, oh dear,
My shoes have great big holes!
Call Schumann's shoe shop
Schumann's new shop,
I need shoes!

I want a pair
To match my yellow hair! **(D.C. al Fine)**

Fine means "the end" or "the finish." It is pronounced "FEEnay."
D. C. al Fine means "go back to the beginning and play to Fine."
The Italian is *da capo al fine*, which means "from the beginning to the end."

CHARLES GOUNOD   (1818 - 1893)

Charles Gounod (goo-NOE) was born in Paris. His father was a painter and his mother a good pianist who gave him lessons. His early compositions were mostly sacred. The *Sanctus* from his best-known Mass, the *Messe solennelle de Saint Cécile*, is one of his most popular sacred compositions. He is chiefly remembered for two operas - *Faust* and *Romeo and Juliet*. The **Funeral March of a Marionette** is a favorite selection for children's concerts. A child told me that the little marionette died because he got tangled in his strings and choked!

Funeral March of a Marionette   [47] & [48]

Gounod, the march of a marionette,
Gounod, the march of a marionette,
Gounod, the funeral march,
The funeral march, the funeral march
Keep on marching!

Gounod, the march of a marionette,
Gounod, the march of a marionette,
Gounod, the puppet died,
And then everyone cried,
But they kept on marching!

Gounod, the march of a marionette,
Gounod, the march of a marionette,
Gounod will lead the band
From his grandstand,
Before everyone disappears!

Gounod, the march of a marionette,
Gounod, the march of a marionette,
Gounod, the puppet died,
And then everyone cried,
But they kept on marching!
GOUNOD!

48

49

JOHANN STRAUSS, JR.
(1825 - 1899)

Johann Strauss, Jr. was called the "Waltz King." It is said that he couldn't dance a waltz, but he certainly could compose one. The waltz was the popular dance of the nineteenth century in Europe, and the Strausses were the favorite composers of the genre. Johann's father was a famous musician and also a composer of beautiful waltzes. His orchestra was the official dance orchestra for Austrian court balls. His father's orchestra played at the coronation ball when Queen Victoria was crowned in England.

Johann Junior played in competition with his father. Vienna was split into two camps, some preferring the father and others the son. When the father died in 1849, Johann Junior took over his father's orchestra. His popularity became even greater than his father's had been.

The waltzes of Johann, Junior are the most famous. *The Blue Danube* is the best-known Strauss waltz, but many of the others are equally delightful. A recording of his waltzes is sure to please you. Unlike a symphony, it does not require your full attention and is great for background music – and for dancing if you know how to waltz!

Strauss also wrote **operettas**, the most popular being *Die Fledermaus* (the flying mouse or *bat!*). It is still a favorite with audiences.

Johann, Junior was like a pop star of today. Women proposed to him or tried to get a lock of his hair. He was married three times!

Johann Strauss became one of the world's best-loved composers. When he died, a whole era came to an end – the end of dancing Vienna.

An **operetta** is a short opera, light and sentimental in character, with some spoken dialogue, music, and dancing.

Blue Danube Waltz

The King of the Waltz, Johann Junior,
The Blue Danube Waltz, J. Strauss, Junior.
Like father, like son, they both composed;
Which one was the best, sure no one knows!

Oh, King of the Waltz, Johann Junior,
The Blue Danube Waltz, J. Strauss Junior.
Yes, fathers and sons come in pairs;
Who's the best, sure no one cares!

51

JOHANNES BRAHMS
(1833 - 1897)

Johannes Brahms is the third member of the "Big Three B's": Bach, Beethoven, and Brahms. They were all German. They fall in alphabetical as well as chronological order, one in each period: Baroque, Classical, and Romantic.

Brahms was another - guess what - musical child prodigy! His family lived in poverty in a crowded tenement on the waterfront of Hamburg, Germany. His father recognized his talent and gave him early training. Little Johannes learned so quickly that he was soon earning some badly needed coins by playing in taverns along the waterfront. Little Johannes hated school, and he often went to bed hungry. However, he loved music. He made up little melodies and wrote them on paper with a kind of musical notation that he had created.

Brahms' music expresses all the rich warmth and expressiveness of the Romantic Period. You won't find as many beautiful melodies in Brahms' music as in Mozart or Chopin. However, Brahms' music has such lush harmony and beauty that you will enjoy listening to it. Once, Brahms autographed a fan for the wife of Johann Strauss. He wrote the melody of *The Blue Danube,* followed by "Unfortunately not by Johannes Brahms."

In the Romantic Period, composers did not find jobs with the church or court. They had to perform, or sell their compositions, or teach (or move in with friends). Fortunately, life was kinder to Johannes as he became older and established his reputation as a composer. Liszt praised him, and Robert and Clara Schumann recognized his genius. The Schumanns were lifelong friends with Brahms and helped his music to become known and published.

Unlike Beethoven, Brahms became rich from the sales of his compositions. More importantly, he was beloved and acclaimed.

Don't play symphonies or concertos as background music. They require your complete attention if you are to enjoy and understand them. Probably only conductors and members of the orchestra really **understand** them. Classical musicians need audiences at their concerts and people to buy their recordings, so they'll be happy if we love classical music and even begin to understand it.

Lullaby

Lullaby, and good night,
Close your eyes now and sleep tight.
Mommy's tired now, Brahms is, too;
Suck your thumb or Daddy's shoe!

Wishing star, waning moon,
Morning sun comes up too soon!
Wishing star, waning moon,
Morning sun comes too soon!

Mom has had it! The baby has been awake half the night, and Mom is desperate for some sleep. She thinks, "Please, Baby, go to sleep! Suck your thumb or your toe or Daddy's shoe, anything that will put you to sleep!"

53

CAMILLE SAINT-SAËNS
(1835 - 1921)

Camille Saint-Saëns (san-SAHNS) was a French composer. To say his name correctly, you have to say it through your nose, but only a Frenchman can really do it right! By now you know that he was probably a child prodigy. When he was two and a half years old, he began piano lessons. He finished his first exercise book in a month and cried for more! He was taught to read musical notation when he was three, and he was composing songs and piano pieces when he was five. When he was only four and a half, he played the piano in a performance of a Beethoven sonata for violin and piano. He went on to become a great organist and composer.

Saint-Saëns' *Carnival of the Animals* is familiar to most children. At Halloween time you may also hear his ***Danse macabre.*** It is a **tone poem** based on a word poem by Henri Cazalis. Saint-Saëns paints a musical picture of the poem. We hear the striking of midnight on the harp; you can count twelve strokes. Then Death tunes his violin, and the dance melody begins. The xylophone was a relatively new instrument in the orchestra. Saint-Saëns used it to depict the rattling of the skeletons' bones. The second theme is quieter as the ghosts float through the air. The dancing pace grows faster and faster until suddenly we hear the cock crow. Dawn has arrived, and the skeletons scurry back to their cold beds. If you listen carefully, you can hear the lids of two coffins bang shut! They will not return until next Halloween.

(You will not hear **all** of the story in the short theme that we are learning. **Classical Magic®** will teach you many short themes. I hope you will like them enough to find recordings of complete works and listen to them.)

Danse macabre is a French title. Notice that danse is spelled with an "s" instead of a "c" as is used in English. Macabre is a French word that means "having death as a subject--ghastly--producing horror."

Danse macabre

(Fiddle tunes up)

[: Danse, macabre danse
  Ghosts and goblins prancing,
  Danse macabre danse,
  Saint-Saëns' goulish song.

Danse, macabre danse
Skeletons are dancing,
Danse, macabre danse
Saint-Saëns' spooky song. :]

The ghosts are floating overhead;
They join in the party,
Can they be dead?
The ghosts are dancing overhead,
I hope they don't tumble down
Into my bed!

GEORGES BIZET
   ## (1838 - 1875)

Georges Bizet (bee-ZAY) was French, another prodigy! He was admitted to the Paris Conservatory to study music when he was only nine. He was the youngest student there, and he stayed for nine years, studying composition and piano. He won many awards for his playing. He is famous principally for his operas. *Carmen* is his most popular opera, but it was not a success when it was first presented. The audience was shocked by a girl smoking on stage and by the sensual story. Later audiences appreciated the wonderful music and were no longer shocked by the story. Unfortunately, Bizet died three months after the opening, so he never knew that it became a big hit. Even today, it is a very popular opera.

The story of Carmen takes place in Spain. However, because Bizet was French, the **libretto** is in French.

The Story of Carmen

Carmen is a gypsy girl who works in a factory in Seville, Spain. She fights with another girl and is arrested. Don José (hoeZAY), an army corporal, is ordered to arrest her, but after she sings *Habanera* and dances, he is charmed by her and lets her escape. He is arrested and put in jail.

A month later, when he gets out of jail, Don José finds Carmen in a tavern with her gypsy friends. She has lost interest in Don José. When Escamillo, the bullfighter, sings his *Toreador*, fickle Carmen falls for him. Zuniga, Don José's boss, also likes Carmen. Don José and Zuniga fight over Carmen. The gypsies force Zuniga to leave. Since Don José has pulled a knife on Zuniga, his commanding officer, he knows he is in trouble. Don José decides to run off with Carmen and the band of gypsies who are smugglers.

Don José is miserable with the gypsies because Carmen ignores him. He leaves when his former girlfriend, Micaela, comes to tell him his mother is dying.

The last scene takes place outside the bullring in Seville. Carmen is now with Escamillo, who is getting ready for a bullfight. Don José finds Carmen, but she tells him to "get lost." Crazy with jealousy, he stabs her in the back saying, "Carmen! My beloved Carmen!" Then he waits to be taken away.

libretto - the words, as distinct from the music, of a musical composition
     such as an opera or an oratorio.
habanera - a Cuban dance in 2/4 syncopated rhythm.
toro - Spanish for "bull."
toreador - Spanish for "bullfighter."

Carmen – Habanera

Bizet
[55] & [56]

[: Habanera, my Carmen dance,
This is the story of a bad romance.
Bizet's Carmen, she lost her life,
Don José stabbed her with a deadly knife. :]

A deadly knife, his deadly knife,
There Carmen lay, poor Don José,
Take him away!
A deadly knife, his deadly knife,
They came and took poor Don José
        Far away!   Olé!

Toreador, be careful of those horns,
They tear you apart and nobody mourns.
Escamillo, wave your banner high.
Carmen is dead, can't you cry?
El toro now is dead, and so is love,
    And so is love,
And so is Carmen's love....................
Toreador, be careful of those horns!
They tear you apart and nobody mourns!

PETER ILYICH TCHAIKOVSKY
(1840-1893)

Peter Ilyich Tchaikovsky (chai-KOV-skee), probably the most famous Russian composer, wrote ballets, symphonies, overtures, concertos, and operas. His ballets are especially captivating for children. Every child loves the music of *Swan Lake*, *Sleeping Beauty* and *The Nutcracker Suite*. You will learn two themes from *Swan Lake* in Volume One of *Themes to Remember*. Tchaikovsky has many other beautiful melodies that you may learn in future volumes.

Tchaikovsky's love of music began early in childhood. He listened to music on a music box and played the melodies on the piano. He began piano lessons when he was five. He was a very sensitive child. Once, going to bed after a concert, he was crying. When asked why he was crying, he said, "The music won't leave my head. It won't let me go to sleep."

He preferred to be by himself, to play the piano, to read or write poetry. As an adult, he was also uncomfortable around other people. One of his greatest friendships was maintained by letters for thirteen years with a person he never met, Madame von Meck.

Tchaikovsky's parents sent him to law school so he'd be able to support himself. Like Schumann, he decided he liked musicians better than lawyers, so he enrolled in music at the St. Petersburg Conservatory in Russia. He ended up broke, as was the case with many musicians. He tried to make money teaching, which wasn't much better. However, he was lucky. A rich widow (Madame von Meck) decided that she loved his music and offered to give him an allowance for the rest of his life. He was free to devote all his time to composing and beautiful music flowed from his pen. Tchaikovsky dedicated his Fourth Symphony to Madame von Meck.

Tchaikovsky's beautiful melodies are enveloped in a rich, romantic warmth. Unlike many composers, he enjoyed recognition and great popularity while he was still living. One of the highlights of his life was conducting his *1812 Overture* at the grand opening of Carnegie Hall in New York City in 1891.

> **suite** - in general terms, a suite is a set of something, like a suite of rooms or a living room suite. In music it refers to a series of instrumental dances as in *The Nutcracker Suite*.

60

Swan Lake - **Theme 1, Waltz**

Swans enchanted, prince and princess,
Swans enchanted on the lake.
Ballet music, dance Tchaikovsky,
Break the spell, love foretell, demoiselle.
Swans enchanted, prince and princess,
Swans enchanted on the lake.
Ballet music, dance Tchaikovsky……

61

Once upon a time there was a handsome young prince named Siegfried. He and his friends were enjoying the evening watching the village people dance. Then his mother appeared.

"Siegfried," she said, "tomorrow is your birthday. You are now a young man, and you must choose a bride at your birthday ball."

Siegfried did not want to think about taking a wife, so he continued to make merry with his friends. As they were walking from the village, they noticed a flight of swans and Siegfried said, "Let us take our bows and enjoy an evening of hunting."

The young men agreed that this would be an exciting adventure, so they followed the flight of the swans into the forest. The swans glided to a lake which reflected the mountains like a mirror.

Siegfried and his friends, with crossbows raised, watched the swans in the moonlight. The young men were spellbound with the beauty of the swans.

Siegfried was ready to shoot his arrow when he saw that the leader of the swans was wearing a crown. Suddenly all the swans were transformed into beautiful maidens. The maiden with the crown was Odette, Queen of the Swans. She told Siegfried her story.

"Rotbart is an evil magician. He has cast a spell upon us. We are swans by day, but we are turned back into maidens at night. The only thing that can break the spell is a man's love, pure and true. Should the man betray us, we will die."

Rotbart had turned himself into a huge owl, and he flew over the maidens to frighten them.

"Don't be frightened," Siegfried said to Odette. "I shall love you forever. You must come to my birthday ball at the castle tomorrow night so that I may present you to my mother and father as my chosen bride."

Odette and Siegfried pledged their love to each other. At dawn, Odette and her friends were again transformed into swans, and they flew away.

64

The next evening at the birthday ball many beautiful maidens were presented to Siegfried, but none of them appealed to him. He could think only of Odette. Suddenly, Rotbart entered with his daughter, Odile, dressed in black. She was disguised to look exactly like Odette. The disguise fooled Siegfried. He danced with Odile and presented her to his parents as his chosen bride.

The ballroom turned dark. Rotbart shrieked, "You can never escape my magic spell. Your kingdom will be mine!"

Rotbart turned into the huge owl and flew out the castle window. Odile smiled at Siegfried, then she also vanished.

Siegfried ran to the castle window and looked out. He could see nothing of Odile or the owl, but he saw a white swan with a crown on her head flying past the castle. He realized that he had been tricked.

Siegfried, frantic with shame and grief, rushed out of the castle and ran to the lake. There he found Odette, surrounded by her friends, sadly crying.

"Odette, my only love, you must forgive me," he said. "I was tricked into betraying you."

Odette could not stop grieving over his unfaithfulness, and she plunged into the lake. Siegfried followed her into the lake, and his sacrifice for love broke Rotbart's evil spell.

The maidens of Swan Lake were never again transformed into swans and Siegfried and Odette were united in eternal love.

Swans swimming on the moonlit lake,
Behold, the fairest wears a crown.
I see the swans changing into maidens fair,
With moon-mist falling in their hair.

Odette the Queen of the Swans so fair
Tells of magic spells, evil spells,
That only love can break!

I see Siegfried coming now.
Will he keep his vow?
Pledge eternal love,
Will he break the spell?…

Swans swimming on the moonlit lake,
Behold, the fairest wears a crown.
I see the swans changing into maidens fair,
With moon-mist falling in their hair.

ANTONIN DVOŘÁK
(1841 - 1904)

Antonin Dvořák (da-VOR-zhak) came from Bohemia, the area later known as the Czech Republic. His childhood was spent among the country folk. His father was a butcher who played the zither for weddings. Antonin played fiddle along with his father, and he learned the songs and dances of his people. He used these melodies in his music which was immediately popular with his countrymen His music is cheerful and full of folk melodies that appeal to all of us.

Dvořák spent three years in New York as a director of the National Conservatory of Music. He was surprised to learn that he was expected to lead the development of an "American" style music. He began by listening to "folk" music. He especially liked the music of African Americans and sang their spirituals with them. Some people said that he used themes from spirituals in the second movement of the *New World* **Symphony**. Dvořák insisted that he composed only in the "spirit" of the music.

Dvořák also visited "middle America." He had a secretary, Josef Kovarik, who had spent his childhood in Spillville, Iowa, a Bohemian community in northeast Iowa. Josef wished to return to his hometown for a visit and he suggested that Dvořák travel with him. Dvořák was happy for the opportunity to visit with American people who spoke his language and knew his culture, so he spent the summer of 1893 in Spillville, Iowa.

Dvořák played the organ in the large Catholic church that his people attended. That organ is still played for the services in the church. There is also a museum in the house where the Dvořák familiy lived that summer. You can see photos of the family and of Chief Big Moon who visited Spillville with his Powwow and Medicine Show. Dvořák was impressed with the Native American music.

It was there in Spillville that Dvořák composed a beautiful string quartet and a string quintet, both known as *the American*. If you ever visit Spillville, Iowa, go to Riverside Park and look for a monument to Dvořák, commemorating his 1893 visit to their town.

Dvořák wrote his *New World* **Symphony No. 9** in honor of his American visit. We think it sounds American, but it is said that his own people think it sounds like Czech music. It is quite an accomplishment to be able to sound Czech-American!

Symphony No. 9 - (*New World*)

Antonin Dvořák, Czech, Bohemian,
New World guest, gave his best,
New World Symphony.
Take me home, take me back;
Friends are calling me.
Mama's there, Papa, too,
My Bohemia!
Antonin Dvořák, Czech, Bohemian,
New World guest, gave his best,
New World Symphony.

EDVARD GRIEG
(1843 - 1907)

Edvard Grieg (GREEG) was the most famous composer of Norway. He lived in a time when many composers felt proud of their countries (nationalism) and were using folk melodies in their classical compositions. Grieg, put the spirit of Norway into his compositions, and the people loved it. The Norwegian government granted him a pension for life. One of his most popular works is the **Peer Gynt Suite**. Grieg wrote this as incidental music for Henrik Ibsen's drama *Peer Gynt*. The story below and the lyrics you will sing are also based on Ibsen's play.

Peer Gynt Suite - Morning   [65] & [66]

Morning is dawning and Peer Gynt is yawning,
But Grieg says, "It's fun to get up, greet the sun!"

Morning is dawning
And Peer Gynt is yawning,
But Grieg says, "It's time
To go visit the trolls!"

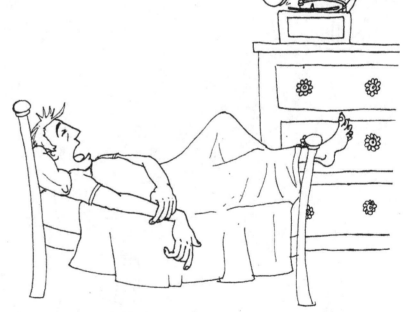

Morning is dawning
And we are all yawning,
But Grieg says,
"Have fun, a new day has
           begun!"

Morning is dawning and Peer Gynt is yawning,
But Grieg says, "It's fun to get up, greet the sun!"

70

Peer Gynt in the Hall of the Mountain King - The Story

Peer Gynt lived in Norway, a land of mountains that rise out of deep blue waters. These mountains are the home of the trolls, strange little people who come out of their caves only after dark.

Peer Gynt was a handsome young man, but he had some very bad habits. He was lazy, he was selfish, and he told lies!

Peer slept late every morning. He wouldn't get out of bed in the morning to help his mother feed the goats and geese. His room was a mess but he didn't care.

Everyone knew that Peer told stories that were not true. Nobody could ever tell whether he was lying or telling the truth.

Peer had decided that he would marry a very pretty girl just his own age. Her name was Solveig. Though Solveig liked Peer very much, she told him he would have to tell the truth or else they could never marry and be happy. "Some day," Solveig said to Peer, "you'll tell a story that will get you into very serious trouble."

Peer just laughed at her. He didn't know how true those words of Solveig's were. She began to cry, but Peer didn't care. He went out for a walk in the woods.

Peer Gynt Suite - Solveig's Song

**Grieg
[67] & [68]**

Peer Gynt, don't you know
That I love you, love you so.
But my sadness will not go.
   I cannot marry you
   If you'll not to me be true.
   You must tell me no more lies.
Great trouble you will find
If the truth you do not mind,
Please change your reckless ways!
   Don't laugh at me that way,
   I love you so,
   But you must know,
   That sadness fills my heart.......

71

Peer Gynt in the Hall of the Mountain King

Grieg
[69] & [70]

While Peer walked he thought about what a handsome, clever fellow he was. "I can say and do anything I please," he thought, "and I'll never get into trouble."

Peer was so busy thinking about how handsome and clever he was that he lost his way in the woods. He walked and walked, frantically trying to find his way out. When night fell, he finally lay down to rest. He heard a strange sound, but he was so tired that he fell asleep. He didn't know that the noise came from the cave of the little troll people. The trolls peeked out of their cave. They ran to ask the Troll King what they should do. He said, "Wait until you are sure that he is sound asleep, then bring him to me, but don't wake him."

They waited until Peer was sound asleep. Then, very slowly, they crept out and formed a circle around him. They lifted him by his legs and arms, carefully so not to wake him, and carried him deep into their cave to the Hall of the Mountain King.

Peer Gynt Suite - In the Hall of the Mountain King   [69] & [70]

Trolls are creeping from the cave,
Some are scared, some are brave.
Peer Gynt sleeps, he doesn't know
They'll take him to their king.

Careful now, please let him sleep.
Take his arms, take his feet.
He will have a big surprise
When he wakes up!

Trolls are creeping from the cave
Faster now, circle round.
Pick him up and take him
To the cave far underground.

Peer Gynt in the Hall of the Mountain King

Grieg]
[69] & [70

Peer awoke as the trolls put him down. There, sitting on a throne, was the King of the Trolls. He looked ugly and mean! Beside him sat the Troll Princess. The Troll King scowled at Peer and said, "Who are you that you dare to come into my forest?"

Peer was frightened. He thought, "I will tell him that I'm a prince. Then he will think I'm an important person and he will let me go."

Acting very brave Peer said, "I am Prince Peer Gynt, son of the King of Norway."

The King of the Trolls believed Peer. He said, "I was going to let you go, but since you are a prince, you will make a fitting husband for my daughter!"

Peer saw the Troll Princess. Although she was smiling at him, she was the ugliest thing he had ever seen. She had sharp teeth, huge ears and hair like cactus.

"I'm no prince," Peer shouted. "I was just telling a story. I'm Peer Gynt, a simple village boy. Can't you see?"

"We will have the wedding in the morning before dawn," said the King.

Then Peer had another idea. "Your daughter is much too lovely for me. She's a princess. I'm sure she wouldn't want me."

But all the trolls shouted, "We'll have the wedding in the morning before dawn!"

Peer Gynt Suite - In the Hall of the Mountain King

Trolls: "Oh great King, we have a prize!
　　　　　We surmise, he's not wise;
　　　　　We have found that he tells lies!
　　　　　What do you advise?"

King: "He shall have my daughter fair,
　　　　　Giant ears, cactus hair.
　　　　　She has lovely pointed teeth;
　　　　　Her face would scare a bear!"

Peer:
"I'm no prince, she won't want me!
　I'm Peer Gynt!
　Can't you see?
　She's too lovely
　For my eyes,
　I'm getting
　　　out of here!"

73

Peer Gynt in the Hall of the Mountain King

The trolls no longer believed Peer. They thought he really was a prince; they wanted him for the Troll Princess.

Peer started running and the angry trolls chased after him. Peer ran faster and faster. He stumbled in the dark. Just as he thought he was free, the trolls grabbed him and held him down. They bound his legs and arms and took him back to the Troll King.

"So, you thought you could get away, did you? Nobody leaves our cave unless we let him go." said the King." You will marry my daughter! We shall prepare for the wedding tonight. We will have the wedding in the morning before dawn!"

All the trolls shouted, "We 'll have the wedding in the morning before dawn.!"

Before Peer knew what had happened to him, he was married to the Troll Princess. It took three years for Peer to find a way to sneak away from the trolls.

Peer Gynt Suite - In the Hall of the Mountain King

King: "You can't leave this cave, my boy.
Think what love, think what joy!
We will have the wedding
In the morning before dawn."

Peer: "I'm no prince, she won't want me!
I'm Peer Gynt! Can't you see?"

King: "We will have the wedding
In the morning before dawn."

Trolls: "We will have the wedding
In the morning before dawn!"

The Happy Couple

Good Listening from the Romantic Period

Rossini:
Messa Di Gloria
Overtures
Quartets for Flute, Clarinet,
    Horn and Bassoon

Saint-Saëns
Carnival of the Animals

Mendelssohn
Capriccio brillant
Violin Concerto in E minor
Songs Without Words

Bizet
Carmen (Highlights)
Symphony No. 1 in C

Chopin
Waltzes, Nocturnes, and Preludes

Tchaikovsky
Violin Concerto in D major
Festival Overture 1812
Piano Concerto No. 1

Brahms
Piano Concerto No. 2 in B-flat
Waltzes and Cello Sonatas

Grieg
Piano Concerto in A minor
Peer Gynt Suites No. 1 and No. 2

Schumann:
Kinderscenen (Scenes from Childhood)
Fantasiestücke (Fantasy Pieces)

Gounod
Sanctus from *Messe Solonelle, St. Cecilia Mass*

Dvořák
String Quartet in F major (*American*)

MODERN

<u>Piano and Forte Go Modern</u>

(1900 to the Present)

Relaxing the Rules

Key Date – 1903
First Flight by the Wright Brothers

THE MODERN PERIOD   (1900 to the Present)

DEBUSSY, Claude	**(1862 - 1918)**
RACHMANINOFF, Sergei	**(1873 - 1943)**
SOUSA, John Philip	**(1854 - 1932)**
ELGAR, Sir Howard	**(1857 - 1934)**

During each period composers try to express themselves in new ways. They break the rules of the previous period and try new forms, harmonies, and rhythms. In the **Modern Period**, composers experimented more than in most periods. For instance, Twentieth Century music includes jazz, electronic music, whole-tone and twelve-tone scale music, and "chance" music.

"Chance" music reminds me of some modern paintings which look like the artist threw paint at the canvas and called the results art. I think some musicians throw notes at the staff, let them land where they may, and then call the result music! John Cage "composed" music by letting four radios, tuned to different stations, play at once. He would also "prepare" the piano for a piece by putting items such as tape, chewing gum, thumb tacks, coins, cloth, and paper on the strings and hammers in order to create new sounds. He wrote one piece called 4'33". The pianist opens the lid of the piano, sits at the keyboard for four minutes and 33 seconds. He then closes the piano without touching a key. I think he must be joking! That would be an easy one for beginners, don't you think? (Although most children can't sit still for four minutes unless they are asleep!) I wonder if some children practice their lessons that way!

Modern music uses a lot more **dissonance** than earlier music. A dissonant sound is one that clashes, which may sound "wrong" to our ears. Jazz music has also influenced modern classical music, but in a wonderful way. Listen to George Gershwin sometime.

Children's ears are usually less bothered by new sounds than are those of adults. They don't have as many preconceived ideas about how music "should" sound.

---

dissonance - sounds that clash, which may sound "wrong" to our ears.

CLAUDE DEBUSSY
(1862 - 1918)

Claude DEBUSSY (de-bu-SEE) from France is said to have started the **Modern Period** with his impressionist style. He creates beauty with impressions rather than with clear images. His melodies create dreamy, misty feelings, like looking at a scene through a fog or in the moonlight. If possible, listen to all of *Clair de lune* while you look at a Monet painting. You will understand impressionism better by listening and looking than by reading.

Debussy was a wonderful pianist who wrote most of his music for the piano. He was known as a musical rebel. He irritated his teachers with the new sounds he produced. He searched for new chords and new scales; he initiated the "whole tone" scale. If you have a piano, start on any key and play every other key (don't forget the black keys) until you decide to stop. You will see how Debussy produced a harp-like sound of misty, moonlight magic. He flunked his music composition course! His teachers certainly didn't expect him to become a famous composer.

Debussy was also a masterful composer for the orchestra. He used innovative combinations of instruments to achieve his delicate sounds. In recordings of his music you will hear the muted horn, the harp glissando, a lonely oboe, and divided string sections over big chords.

Debussy wrote music for his only daughter, known as Chouchou. He composed a children's ballet for her, *La Boïte á joujoux* (The Box of Toys), and a suite for the piano called, *The Children's Corner*. He used English titles for the entire work to suggest an English governess caring for a French child.

There are six sections:
Doctor Gradus ad Parnassum - a child struggling with piano exercises
Jimbo's Lullaby - Jimbo being a toy elephant
Serenade of the Doll
The Snow is Dancing
The Little Shepherd
Golliwogg's Cake Walk - with strutting rhythms of the popular American cakewalk

Clair de lune   (Moonlight)

Sing with me, Debussy.
Sing of the moonlight, Clair de lune,
Love's song enchanting
Capturing, enrapturing me!
Love song bewitching,
Leaving me---longing for---you!
Sing with me, Debussy,
Lovely music, misty moon,
        Ah…………...

SERGEI RACHMANINOFF
(1873 - 1943)

Sergei Rachmaninoff (rock-MAHN-in-off) was Russian, born in the **Romantic Period** but lived well into the **Modern Period**. We might expect him to compose in the modern mode, but he was a Romantic at heart. His music is lush and richly warm; his melodies soar, and his piano music is rhapsodic. Tchaikovsky knew him and had a great influence on his music. He was not the usual child prodigy. He did not become really serious about music until he entered the Moscow Conservatory at age fifteen. In addition to piano he studied composition. He won the Great Gold Medal for composition which had been awarded only twice in the history of the conservatory. When he was only eighteen and still in school, he composed his First Piano Concerto.

Rachmaninoff, with his wife and two daughters, left Russia at the time of the Russian Revolution of 1917, never to return to his country. He was a virtuoso pianist and traveled the world giving concerts. He specialized in the music of Chopin in addition to his own. He moved to the United States in 1935. A few weeks before he died he became a citizen of the U.S.

He composed mostly for the piano. His concertos are very difficult to play. Musicians call him "Rocky" and they call his Second Piano Concerto "Rocky Two." You will learn a beautiful theme from the third movement of this concerto. His Third Piano Concerto is called - that's right - "Rocky Three." It is incredibly difficult. It is the concerto that tormented David Helfgott, (twentieth century classical pianist) to the point of a nervous breakdown (as portrayed in the 1996 movie *Shine).*

Rachmaninoff recorded many of his own works so we can listen to the master himself.

Piano Concerto No. 2 - Mvt. 3

Rachmaninoff
[73] & [74]

Sergei Rachmaninoff,
I want to wrap your music
'Round me like a shawl,
And I shall wear
Your great Concerto Two
To warm me, cheer me,
Inspire me to live
And to love and to dream.......
Sergei Rachmaninoff,
I want to wrap your music
'Round me like a shawl.

JOHN PHILIP SOUSA
(1854 - 1932)

John Philip Sousa (SUE-za) is America's best-remembered and favorite bandmaster. He wrote more than a hundred marches that are still favorites. He is known as the "March King." We will learn the themes for *Semper Fidelis* and *The Stars and Stripes Forever.* When he was twelve, he planned to run away to join the circus. When his father found out about John's plan, he arranged for him to be an apprentice in the United States Marine Band. That kept him at home and happy. He knew how to play the violin, piano, and various wind instruments. When he was twenty-six, he was appointed leader of the Marine Band. He turned it into a band of perfection, both in performance and in appearance.

In 1892 Sousa decided to form his own concert band. The band toured Europe four times. He played his own marches and introduced Europeans to America's **ragtime music**. Scott Joplin, an African American composer, developed the piano style called ragtime.

In his tours of the United States, Souza introduced people to the music of Tchaikovsky, Dvořák, Rossini, and Suppé, in addition to his own compositions.

A **sousaphone** is a type of tuba with a wide "bell" that can be turned to throw the sound in different directions. It was named after John Philip because it was his idea.

Sousa wrote an autobiography called *Marching Along.*

Ragtime music - jazzy, syncopated music that was played on pianos in honky-tonks. What is a honky-tonk? You could ask your great-grandmother, but she might not tell you if she knows. Mr. Webster says that a honky-tonk is a "cheap, noisy, garish nightclub or dance hall." (Sometimes ragtime pianists played classical music in a ragtime style. This was called "ragging the classics.")

Scott Joplin wrote and played wonderful ragtime music. You may have heard his *Maple Leaf Rag* or *The Entertainer.*

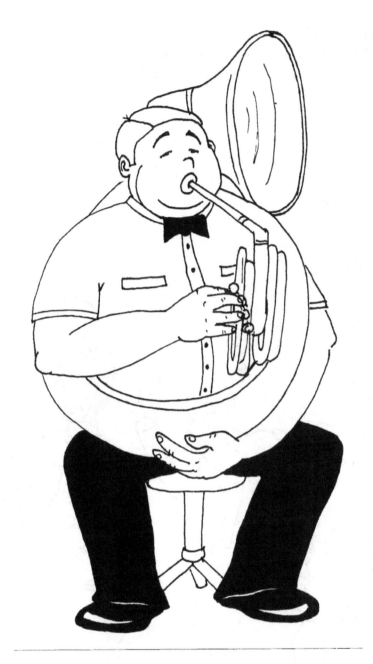

Playing the Sousaphone

Stars and Stripes Forever

Hail to the Stars and the Stripes!
May this symbol of peace be forever.
Step high, beat the drums, wave the flag.
John Philip Sousa, the King of the March!

Oh, hail to the Stars and the Stripes!
May this symbol of peace be forever.
Step high, beat the drums, wave the flag!
King of the March, King of the March,
John Philip Sousa!

Semper Fidelis

Semper Fidelis march, march down the street,
Always faithful to keep the beat,
Sousa wants you to keep the beat!
Please stop all of the traffic coming down the street.
Stop! Don't you dare to interfere with our parade!

Semper Fidelis march, march down the street,
Always faithful to keep the beat,
Sousa wants you to keep the beat!
Please stop all of the traffic coming down the street.
Stop! And if you should get in the way, we'll call a cop! Stop!

semper - always, ever.
fidelis - faithful.   (Both are Latin words.)

87

SIR EDWARD ELGAR
(1857 - 1934)

Sir Edward Elgar was English, as you may have guessed by the "Sir." To be called by the title "Sir," a man must be "knighted" by the sovereign. Elgar was knighted in 1904 in recognition of his contribution to English music.

When Queen Victoria died in 1901 her eldest son became King Edward VII. Elgar was asked to provide music for Edward's coronation. He composed *Pomp and Circumstance.* It is music made for ceremonies and great occasions. That is why you will hear it at almost every grade school, high school, and college graduation.

Elgar composed violin and cello concertos and two symphonies. He also composed a work known as the *Enigma* Variations. (An enigma is a puzzle.) There were fourteen variations. Each variation, except the last, was dedicated to a friend. He dedicated the last variation to himself. According to Elgar, there is a theme that underlies the whole work. The puzzle or "enigma" is this: What is the underlying theme?

Elgar produced many fine works, two symphonies, the Concerto for Violin and Orchestra, several oratorios, several concert overtures, and chamber-music works. At the height of his success as a composer, he suddenly would write no more. His beloved wife had died and it destroyed his will to create.

For ten years Elgar did not compose. Finally in 1934 he wrote a hymn of prayer for the recovery of George V, then seriously ill. He had decided that he would work again and began writing his third symphony. However, he did not live to complete it as he underwent surgery for a tumor and never recovered.

While Elgar is a composer of the **Modern Period,** his music is not dissonant. He is more of the conservative tradition of Brahms and Schumann. He has a gift for creating melodies, and his music is warm and skillfully crafted.

88

Pomp and Circumstance

March in great celebration,
Pomp and circumstance rule.
Elgar wrote this procession
For graduating from school!
Elgar wrote this procession
For graduating from school!

Good Listening from the Modern Period

Debussy
Prelude to the Afternoon of a Faun
La Mer (The Sea)

Rachmaninoff
Piano Concerto No. 2 in A minor
Rhapsody on a Theme of Paganini

John Philip Sousa
Stars and Stripes Forever
Semper Fidelis
King Cotton
The Washington Post
El Capitan

Elgar
Pomp and Circumstance
Enigma Variations

Gershwin
Rhapsody in Blue
American in Paris

Copland
Appalachian Spring
Billy the Kid
Rodeo
El salón México

Coates
The Three Elizabeths
Four Centuries
The Three Bears
London Suite

APPENDIX 1---MUSICAL NOTATION

BAROQUE

Vivaldi--*Four Seasons* --*Spring*   [1] & [2]

Bach--Toccata & Fugue in D minor--Theme 1   [3] & [4]

Bach--Toccata & Fugue in D minor--Theme 2   [5] & [6]

Handel--*WaterMusic*--*Alla Hornpipe*   [7] & [8]

APPENDIX 1

BAROQUE

Handel--*Hallelujah* Chorus   [9] & [10]

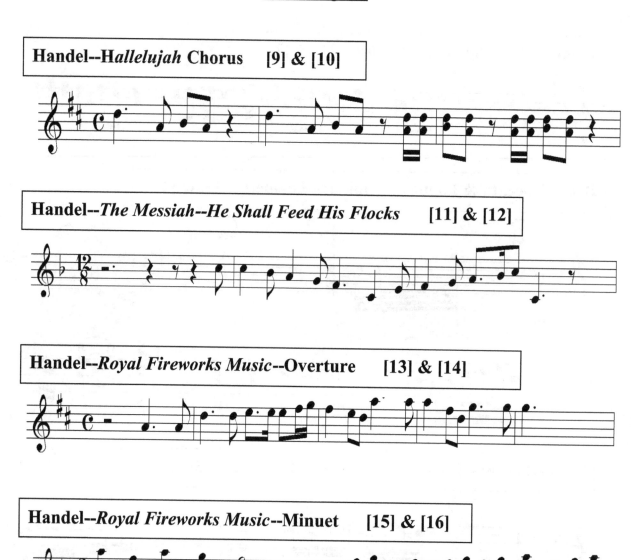

Handel--*The Messiah--He Shall Feed His Flocks*   [11] & [12]

Handel--*Royal Fireworks Music*--Overture   [13] & [14]

Handel--*Royal Fireworks Music*--Minuet   [15] & [16]

Handel--*Royal Fireworks Music--La Paix*   [17] & [18]

CLASSICAL

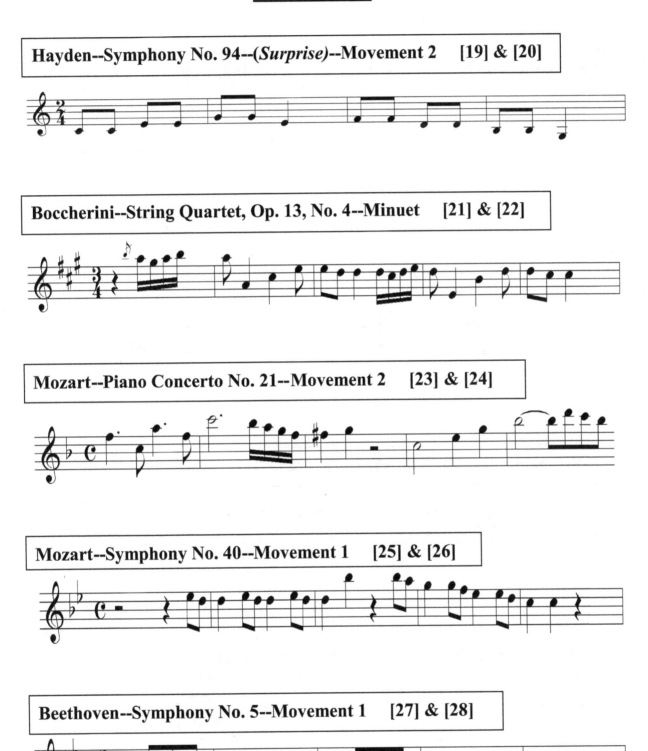

Hayden--Symphony No. 94--(*Surprise*)--Movement 2   [19] & [20]

Boccherini--String Quartet, Op. 13, No. 4--Minuet   [21] & [22]

Mozart--Piano Concerto No. 21--Movement 2   [23] & [24]

Mozart--Symphony No. 40--Movement 1   [25] & [26]

Beethoven--Symphony No. 5--Movement 1   [27] & [28]

APPENDIX 1

CLASSICAL

Beethoven--Symphony No. 9--Movement 4   [29] & [30]

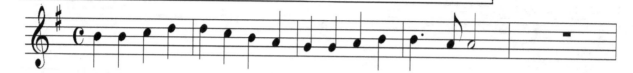

Beethoven--Sonata No. 4--(*Moonlight*)   [31] & [32]

Schubert--Symphony No. 8--(*Unfinished*)--[33] & [34]

Schubert--Piano Quintet in A--(*The Trout*))   [35] & [36]

MUSICAL NOTATION (Continued)

ROMANTIC

Rossini--*William Tell Overture*--Theme 1   [37] & [38]

Rossini--*William Tell Overture*--Theme 2, *Trumpet Fanfare*   [39] & [40]

Mendelssohn--*A Midsummer Night's Dream*--*Wedding March*   [41] & [42]

Chopin--*Grand valse Brillante*   [43] & [44]

Schumann--*The Happy Farmer*   [45] & [46]

APPENDIX 1

ROMANTIC

Gounod--*Funeral March of a Marionette*   [47] & [48]

Strauss--*Blue Danube Waltz*   [49] & [50]

Brahms--*Lullaby*   [51] & [52]

Saint-Saëns--*Danse Macabre*   [53] & [54]

MUSICAL NOTATION (Continued)

ROMANTIC

Bizet--Carmen--*Habanera*   [55] & [56]

Bizet--Carmen--*Toreador*   [57] & [58]

Tchaikovsky--*Swan Lake*--Theme 1   [59] & [60]

Tchaikovsky--*Swan Lake*--Theme 2   [61] & [62]

APPENDIX 1

ROMANTIC

Dvořák--Symphony No. 9--(New World)   [63] & [64]

Grieg--*Peer Gynt Suite--Morning*   [65] & [66]

Grieg--*Peer Gynt Suite--Solveig's Song*   [67] & [68]

Grieg--*Peer Gynt Suite--In the Hall of the Mountain King*   [69] & [70]

MODERN

Debussy--*Clair de Lune*   [71] & [72]

Rachmaninoff--Piano Concerto No. 2--Movement 3   [73] & [74]

Sousa--*Stars and Stripes Forever*   [75] & [76]

Sousa--*Semper Fidelis*   [77] & [78]

Elgar--*Pomp and Circumstance*   [79]& [80]

APPENDIX 2

GLOSSARY

allegro - Fast tempo.

arpeggio -The notes of a chord played one at a time instead of together.

ballet - A theatrical performance using ballet dancing to convey
a story, theme, or atmosphere.

baroque - The historical period (c.1600 - 1750) where music and art were
ornate, exuberant, and dynamic.

bourrée - A French 17th century dance, or the music for that dance
in quick duple meter.

band - An instrumental group composed principally of woodwind,
brass, and percussion instruments.

cantata - A choral composition with choruses and solos,
usually accompanied by organ, piano, or orchestra.

chord - A musical sound made when three or more notes are
played at the same time.

coda - A concluding musical section that is formally distinct
from the main structure, an added ending.

classical - Refers to music that is more complex and is
more enduring than popular music.

classical magic - A magical way to remember classical music, themes, and composers.

concert band - Sometimes called a "symphonic band."
It is larger than a pep band or a smaller town band
and has more classical music in its repertory.

concerto - A composition for a full orchestra featuring a solo
instrument. Usually three movements   Fast   Slow   Fast.

da capo al fine - Italian meaning " from the beginning to the end."

D. C. al Fine - Go back to the beginning and play to Fine (FEE nay),
i.e. to the end, or to the finish.

APPENDIX 2

demoiselle - A French word for "young lady."

dissonant - A sound that clashes, which may sound "wrong" to our ears.

étude - A study , a piece aimed at teaching a musical skill.

finale - The final part of a musical work.

fine - (FEEnay) - The end.

forte - Loud, strong.

fugue - A "round" written for instruments.

grace note - An extra note played very quickly before the main note.

gavotte - A French dance in moderate 4/4 time.

habanera - A Cuban dance in 2/4 syncopated rhythm.

hornpipe - An English folk clarinet having one ox horn concealing the reed and another
forming the bell. It also gave its name to a dance related to the Irish jig. It features
hopping and kicking of the feet. It became popular with sailors because it could be
done in a small space without a partner.

impromptu - A composition of the Romantic Period. The name implies a somewhat casual
origin of the piece in the composer's mind.
improvise - To make up new music on the spur of the moment.

la paix - (la pay) Peace in French.

libretto - The written words of a musical work such as an opera or an oratorio.

mazurka - A lively Polish dance in triple meter (three beats).

measure - A basic unit of musical time, usually containing two, three, or four beats.

minuet - A slow, stately dance in triple meter (3 beats). It evolved into the waltz of
the romantic Period.

motive - Similar to a theme only much shorter.

movement - A distinct part of a musical composition, like a chapter in a book.
Musicians will usually stop completely between movements.

nocturne - A dreamy composition appropriate for nighttime.

omnipotent - Almighty or infinite in power.

opera - A musical play with orchestra, chorus, solos, and people in costume who sing
      rather than speak their lines.

operetta - A short opera, light, and sentimental in character, with some spoken
      dialogue, music, and dancing.

Op. - Abbreviation for Opus.

Opus - A *work*. It is used by composers and publishers to identify their works.
      The word is usually reserved for a collection of works of the same kind.
      Op. 13, No. 4 would mean that the music is No. 4 in Book 13.

oratorio - A musical story, usually from the Bible, with soloists, chorus and
      orchestra. All the words are sung but nobody dresses in costumes or acts
      the parts. Handel's *Messiah* is an oratorio.

orchestra - A group of instrumentalists, especially string players, organized to play music
      together.

overture - An instrumental composition meant as an introduction to an
      opera, oratorio, or similar work. Some overtures stand by themselves,
      such as *The 1812 Overture* by Tchaikovsky.

piano - Quiet, soft.

piano quintet - Usually consists of a piano and a string quartet which has two violins, one viola
      and one cello.

polonaise - A stately Polish processional dance in triple meter.

polyphonic - Music which has two or more melodies played at the same time.

prelude - A small concert piece based on a short motive.

quartet - A composition for four instruments or voices.

quintet - A composition written for five instruments. A quintet can be made
      up of any five instruments.

recitative - Music which sounds almost like speaking – used in operas and oratorios.

APPENDIX 2

romantic - Showing feeling, emotion.

scherzo - Italian word for "joke." The music is rollicking as the
        name suggests. Has triple meter. (Count 1 -2 -3).

semper fidelis - Always, ever faithful. (Both are Latin words.)

sight-read - To read and play music that one has never seen or practiced before.

sonata - composition for only one or two instruments.
        Usually three movements   Fast Slow Fast.

sonata - A composition for only one or two instruments.
        Usually three movements   Fast Slow Fast.

string quartet - A composition for two violins, viola and cello.
        Usually four movements   Fast Slow Minuet Fast.

string quintet - A composition for two violins, two violas and one cello.

suite - In general terms, a suite is a set of something, like a suite of rooms
        or a living room suite. In music it refers to a series of instrumental
        dances as in *The Nutcracker Suite.*

symphony - A composition for a full orchestra.
        Usually four movements   Fast Slow Minuet Fast.

        (Symphony can also refer to the type of orchestra that plays symphonies.)

syncopated - Music in which the weak beat is accented - jazz music uses it a lot.
        If you think it sounds jazzy, it's probably syncopated!

tête-á-tête - Face to face.

theme - A musical idea that is developed in a composition.

toccata - A keyboard composition played (touched) very fast. Toccata
        comes from the Italian word *toccare* which means "to touch."

tone poem - A poem in music rather than words.

toro - Spanish for "bull."

toreador - Spanish for "bullfighter."

trill - The quick repeating of two adjacent notes.

trio - A composition for three instruments or voices.

triple - Having three units or members.

variation - The repetition of a musical theme with
modifications in rhythm, tune, harmony, or key.

virtuoso - A performer who excels on his or her musical instrument.

waltz - A lively couple dance with three beats in a measure.

BIBLIOGRAPHY

Apel, Willi. *Harvard Dictionary of Music.* Cambridge: Harvard University Press, 1972.

Barlow, Harold and Morgenstern, Sam. *A Dictionary of Musical Themes.* New York: Crown, 1948.

Cross, Milton and Ewen, David. *Encyclopedia of the Great Composers and Their Music.* New York: Doubleday, 1953.

The Earl of Harewood and Peattie, Antony. *The New Kobbé's Opera Book.* New York: G.P. Putnam's Sons, 1922, 1997.

Ewen, David. *Encyclopedia of Concert Music.* New York: Hill and Wang, 1959.

Gmoser, Lulu Britz. *Great Composers.* New York: Smithmark, 1997.

Grout, Donald Jay. *The History of Western Music.* New York: W.W. Norton, 1960.

Hampton Miniature Arrow Scores, Volume 5, *The Ballets of Igor Stravinsky.*

Kamien, Roger. *Music, An Appreciation.* New York: McGraw-Hill, 1998.

Koolbergen, Jeroen. *Vivaldi.* New York: Smithmark, 1996.

Lloyd, Norman. *The Golden Encyclopedia of Music.* New York: Golden Press, 1968.

Pogue, David, and Speck, Scott. *Opera for Dummies.* Foster City, California: IDG Books Worldwide, 1997.

Pogue, David, and Speck, Scott. *Classical Music for Dummies.* Foster City, California: IDG Books Worldwide, 1997.

The Columbia Encyclopedia, Fifth Edition. New York: Houghton Mifflin, 1993.

INDEX OF CD TRACKS

INDEX OF COMPOSERS

INDEX OF COMPOSITIONS

CPSIA information can be obtained
at www.ICGtesting.com
Printed in the USA
JSHW020458200720
6751JS00004B/54